the **whimsical**bake**house**

the
whimsical

bakehouse

FUN-TO-MAKE CAKES THAT TASTE AS GOOD AS THEY LOOK!

Kaye Hansen and Liv Hansen
photographs by Ben Fink

FOREWORD BY MEREDITH VIEIRA

Clarkson Potter/Publishers
New York

For Luiz and Peter

**And in memory of Liv's father, Johnny,
who unknowingly played his part in this creation.**

Library of Congress Cataloging-in-Publication Data
Hansen, Kaye.
    The whimsical bakehouse : fun-to-make cakes that taste as good as they
  look / by Kaye Hansen and Liv Hansen ; photographs by Ben Fink
        p. cm.
    Includes index.
    1. Cake decorating. 2. Cake. I. Hansen, Liv. II. Title.

    TX771.2.H35 2002
    641.8'653—dc21   2001054853

ISBN 978-0-307-58754-1

Printed in China

Design by Caitlin Daniels Israel

10 9 8 7 6 5 4 3 2 1

First Paperback Edition

Acknowledgments

If it weren't for our friend and loyal customer Felicity Nitz, we would never have met Carla Glasser, whose determination made this book possible. Thank you both. Many thanks to our editor, Pam Krauss, for her guidance, and to Ben Fink, whose creative input helped bring our vision to life. We are grateful to everyone who tested our recipes at home, sampled our treats, proofread our notes, and assisted us at work: Pam, Katherine, and Meagan Heus; Mary Hudson; Julie Baiardi; Jen Monette; the Bakehouse staff; and of course our husbands, Luiz Silva and Peter Simon.

Contents

Foreword

I was looking for a birthday cake for my daughter, Lily, when I first wandered into the Riviera Bakehouse. She was having a "fairy princess" party, and I wanted something special—after all, your little girl doesn't turn three every day. As I opened the bakery door that cold January afternoon, there was the gentle tinkle of a bell overhead, followed by a wave of warmth. Warm sticky buns, cookies, coffee, and Kaye, the shop's owner and also the mother of her own little girl, now all grown up.

"I'd like a fairy princess cake," I said, nibbling the toe of a buttery bear-shaped cookie. Kaye smiled at me in the way of a mother who understands the importance of princesses and parties and turning three.

"Let me get my daughter, Liv," Kaye said, her words trailing off as she disappeared into the kitchen. A few moments later a lovely young woman appeared, lightly dusted in flour.

"I'd like a fairy princess cake," I said again, realizing how silly I must sound. But Liv just grinned shyly, the way girls do who understand magic and make-believe. She asked me Lily's favorite colors (pink and purple) and sent me back out into the afternoon on a shopping expedition. Take Lily and find a little doll that looks like her, I was told.

And we did. I returned to the Riviera Bakehouse a few days later and dropped off the plastic doll with long brown hair and shiny eyes. Liv poked her head out of the kitchen just long enough to flash that grin.

The morning of February 7, Lily put on her leotard and tutu. She grabbed a wand covered in silver glitter and announced that today was her birthday and she was a fairy princess. As we waited for her friends to arrive, I drove to the Riviera. Once again I was greeted by the tinkle of the bell and the wave of warmth. My eyes met Kaye's, and she nodded in the direction of a large cooler. I turned my head, and stared breathless through the frosty glass. Lily's plastic doll had been transformed into a princess, dressed in a flowing gown of cake covered in buttercream. It was as if she'd been plucked from the pages of a fairy tale and made real.

Liv emerged just long enough for me to embarrass her. "You're not a cake decorator, you're an artist! You should be working in New York City. Do you know how successful you would be? I've never seen such beautiful work!" I was still going on as Liv assured me she was quite happy where she was and was pleased I loved the cake. And then she excused herself and went back to her work.

I'll never forget the look on Lily's face that afternoon when I threw open the doors to the dining room and she and her friends gazed upon her birthday cake. She stood there in her tutu, her silver wand at her side and her mouth wide open. How do you thank someone for giving your child such a moment of wonderment?

Liv, this is my way of thanking you. I want everyone who picks up this book to know that what you spin so beautifully is not just sugar. It's magic.

Ever since that cold day in January five years ago, I have wandered into the Riviera Bakehouse more times than my waistline cares to admit. Reader, if you ever find yourself in Ardsley, New York, you too must make your way to the source, because, as lovely as this book is, it's just a sampling. You'll know you're there by the tinkle of the bell, the wave of warmth, and Kaye's smile, not to mention that of her wonderful husband, Peter. Oh, yes, and the magic words: "Let me get my daughter, Liv."

—Meredith Vieira

Introduction

Liv: The cakes we make at the Bakehouse represent a melding of two sensibilities: my mom's passion for baking unforgettably delicious desserts and my own desire to create whimsical and delightful treats for the eye.

        Kaye: Liv's cakes offer a refreshing change from more serious, traditional decorating. Her designs are simultaneously carefree and beautiful, with a playful quality.

Liv: Just like every bite of your cakes is at once decadent enough to satisfy the most sophisticated palate and yummy enough to placate the child in all of us. The rich Chocolate Butter Cake with absolutely yummy Cookies and Cream filling is a perfect example.

        Kaye: I never fail to marvel at what Liv devises. She says it's because I'm her mom that I'm so amazed by her work, but the delighted reactions of our customers tell the real story. She took what I taught her to new heights.

Liv: From the time I was a little girl I watched my mother bake, knit, spin, weave, and sew and as I grew she shared this knowledge with me, letting me experiment in the kitchen, teaching me the crafts she had learned, helping me knit and reknit my first sweater, guiding me through my first quilt, and nurturing my interest in art. In turn, I became my mom's aesthetic consultant, from choosing the color of paint for the living room to designing her first business card. We found we loved working together on projects large and small, and that our best creations were those we did together.

        Kaye: Most of my childhood memories revolve around baking. I am the fourth of ten children (seven girls and three boys), so needless to say my mother spent a lot of time in the kitchen. All her baking was from scratch: twelve birthday cakes a year (usually Pinwheel Cake, page 84), sticky buns and Parker House rolls every Sunday, all of our Thanksgiving pies, stollen and cutout cookies at Christmas,

the Paschal Lamb at Easter, and cream puffs whenever, just because they were our favorite. I loved to watch her, and the whole process of baking fascinated me. So it's not really surprising that Liv and I have ended up in the kitchen together, too.

Liv: Baking has always been a part of our lives, although for you it started out more as a hobby than an avocation. Growing up I never had store-bought bread, and as I look back I am amazed how you always found time to bake— even though, as a single mom, you worked more than one job to support us. There was always a jar of natural starter in the fridge, and when you made bread I loved to punch down the dough after it rose. As unhappy as I was then about school lunches made on oatmeal onion dill or whole wheat bread, I now recognize what an effort that represented—and how lucky I was!

Kaye: From bread it was a natural extension to begin baking sweeter things. I started with quick breads; Almond Tea Bread from the *Sunset Bread Book* was a favorite. I quickly moved on to more adventurous baking— tarts, cookies, and, of course, cakes. People seemed to like them, and before I knew it, I was getting requests for special occasion cakes.

Liv: I remember the first wedding cake you made. It was simple and elegant with little pearl dots and marzipan roses. The inside was layers of Chocolate Butter and Yellow Butter Cake filled with raspberry jam, the same recipes you use today.

Kaye: I let you have the scraps, which you made into a miniature tiered cake with its own tiny pink flowers on each layer. The bride placed it next to the big cake at the reception. Even at the age of ten you must have had some premonition of your future career.

Liv: That first attempt at baking on a larger scale turned out to be the start of a whole new career in catering and baking.

Kaye: And you were my most reliable assistant, not only in preparing but also serving at the events. Before I knew it you were helping me decorate the cakes I baked for these occasions. It was clear you had a real flair for cake design, and from the time you were twelve until you went to college you made all of my buttercream roses.

Liv: We get a good laugh looking at photographs of our early, rather primitive cakes. Crooked, but not on purpose, and my silly little squiggly attempts at filigree everywhere. You know what? I still love squiggles and swirls.

Kaye: The Riviera Bakehouse (then the Riviera Bakery) had been in existence for forty years when my husband and I took over, and though we kept many of their old standbys, we added many new things—especially more decorative cakes. But it was when Liv claimed the decorating room as her own that I started to notice customers coming in just to see what she might have created that week. Liv learned on the job, and each week she would make a new cake, trying out some new design or technique.

Liv: I learned how essential experimentation with media and techniques is to artistic growth while studying painting, so I am accustomed to trying out new materials and ideas. I felt free to be experimental with my decorations because I knew that my mom's cakes would be delicious no matter how I embellished them.

Kaye: Every week we highlight a theme cake that is related to the season, like Summer Nights with twinkling lightning bugs and a glowing full moon when the weather turns warm, or Winter Wonderland with its icy landscape when we have our first snowfall. When we started working together at the Bakehouse, we discovered that we shared a decorating philosophy—in addition to being beautiful, we think everything on the cake should be edible, and not only edible, but scrumptious.

Liv: I never liked gum paste flowers because even though they are beautifully crafted, their wire centers are not exactly appetizing. After all, a cake is a cake, and in the end it should and will be eaten— I don't even like putting wooden dowels in tiered cakes! I also delight in a quirky balance of perfection and imperfection, so that even a design that is quite detailed will still look handmade and edible.

Kaye: I think that what makes our cakes most special is Liv's chocolate decorations. She has developed a way to make ornaments for cakes that are amazing, fanciful, childlike, dreamy, and amusing. And most people (Liv being an exception) love chocolate.

Liv: The chocolate method was a serendipitous discovery that came about from my desire to expand the limits of cake decorating beyond the traditional techniques. I had been working directly on the cakes but wanted to have more flexibility and work more efficiently, as well as find a way to make freestanding elements that would give the cakes more dimension. I knew from making roses that buttercream froze well and in that state it could be handled for a few seconds. I piped a Christmas stocking stuffed with presents onto a piece of parchment paper and placed it in the freezer; when it was completely hardened I peeled the design off the paper and applied it to a cake before it softened. Next, I tried making small items in chocolate, which led to the discovery of a new technique, my first creation being a strawberry. Using melted chocolate to outline the form, pits, and leaves, I then filled in with red and green buttercream. This greatly expanded the possibilities for freestanding decorations, but it was not perfect. Large designs broke easily and rich colors would sweat after being frozen. I tried using uncolored white wafer chocolate (also called confectioners' chocolate) to flood the chocolate drawings, but I missed color.

Kaye: You tried the powdered colors I used to tint icings but they didn't always dissolve fully in the chocolate, and the colors weren't saturated. Then while flipping through one of our baking supply catalogs we noticed the oil-based gel colors that candy makers use to color their confections. You were so excited, it was like finding the key to the lock; they let you create colorful and detailed designs that could be handled easily.

Liv: The techniques in this book are the result of our years of working together and reflect the most tried-and-true (and best received!) cakes that we have come up with so far.

Kaye: Liv has found a way to keep our creations fun and whimsical and I continue to find joy in creating cakes that are equally memorable for their taste. We hope the cakes on the pages that follow will inspire you to be bold, do the unexpected, and most important—have fun!

How to Get Started

This book is composed of three sections: "The Basics," "Simple Cakes," and "Tiered Cakes." For the best results, we suggest you familiarize yourself with "The Basics" before starting in on any of the cakes. This section contains essential information on tools, ingredients, baking, and cake assemblage that will be helpful whether you are making a cake for a small get-together or a large-scale celebration. Here's where you'll find information about basic icings, mixing icing colors, and more.

The next section introduces relatively straightforward cakes, those with just a single tier and involving fewer decorative techniques. Each of these cakes illustrates a different technique that we use at the Bakehouse and is accompanied by one or more recipes that we feel suit the design. You'll find that the decorating techniques become more demanding as you progress through the section but all of these are suitable for beginners. The final section presents the tiered cakes. We consider these cakes more advanced because they combine two or more decorating techniques and require multiple batches of batter, fillings, and icing. Still, if taken step by step, even these most elaborate cakes are within the abilities of a motivated beginner.

At the end of the book you will find useful information regarding baking times and pan sizes, guidelines for yields (both in standard-size servings and smaller wedding portions), and resources.

For every project in this book we have recommended one or more cake recipes and fillings, but don't feel limited by these suggestions; if your guest of honor loves carrot cake or you're baking for a dedicated chocoholic, go ahead and replace the recommended cake with another of your choice, and pair it with a complementary filling.

To make it easier to substitute, we've noted each recipe's yield in cups; that way, if your preferred recipe's yield is less (or greater) than what is yielded by the recipe we have suggested, you can adjust the number of batches required to make the cake as pictured.

All the cakes in this book were decorated with one of two mediums: tinted buttercream icing, applied either with a spatula or a pastry bag and tip, or freestanding designs made of melted and tinted chocolate. Many incorporate both buttercream and chocolate designs and the most complex cakes may use three or more decorating techniques.

The chocolate designs vary in complexity, ranging from simple, single-color decorations to designs outlined in one color and filled in with one or more additional colors. The most intricate designs are outlined, then subtly shaded with multiple colors that are applied with a paintbrush; this technique is a combination of a traditional cake decorating process known as the run method and the principles of candy making, in which designs are generally built in reverse (from detail to background) and then turned out—or in this case, reversed—to reveal the finished design. (Think of your chocolate Easter bunny, with its pink nose, white eyes, and a purple ribbon around its neck. The colors were painted or piped into the mold before it was filled with chocolate.) The basic ingredients for chocolate decorations, too, are borrowed from the candy maker's craft: white and dark chocolate and candy-tinting colors.

Unlike the run method, in which designs are outlined directly onto a cake and then filled in with melted buttercream (a time-consuming and temperamental procedure that requires that the buttercream be perfect lest it break down when melted or drip off the side of the cake) chocolate designs can be mass-produced on a sheet pan and applied to the cake in any way the baker desires. You can make one or make dozens and even store them for several weeks if you like. Because they are chocolate they will still taste and look great.

Although we are professional bakers, neither my mom nor I had any professional training, and you don't need it either; the methods we use are strictly homespun. You'll find the ingredients and tools needed to make chocolate designs are easily accessible from a well-stocked bakers' supply store or via mail order and are easy to work with. The cake and filling recipes are straightforward and have all been prepared using standard home equipment. Throughout the book you'll find tips from us both based on the lessons we've learned through trial and error, Kaye from the perspective of having baked countless cakes of every size and shape and me with the experience of having worked my way through untold gallons of melted chocolate and buttercream to perfect my decorating skills. With a little practice and a willingness to let loose, you will be baking and decorating fun and delicious cakes of your own in no time.

—Liv Hansen

part one
THE BASICS

No matter how elaborate or relatively unadorned you choose to make your creation, there are a few fundamental steps that apply to each and every cake in this book. These are the basics, and unless you're baking your batter in a sheet pan and serving un-iced hunks right out of the pan—hey, even we have been known to do that on occasion—you'll be using these techniques each time you tie on the apron and get out the pastry bag

Knowing the tools of the trade, learning how to work with chocolate, mix color, and assemble cakes—these are the foundation for making a decorated cake, whether a petite six-incher or a four-tiered wedding cake. So as tempting as it is to skip right to the recipes, please read through this section and get comfortable with the techniques gathered here. It will make every project you attempt go more smoothly.

Tools of the Trade

The basic tools of cake decorating are quite simple and pleasingly low-tech; none requires electricity and few have moving parts. Obtaining some will require a trip to a cake decorating or baking supply store, but many can be found at houseware, craft, or even hardware stores. If you can't get what you need locally, virtually all of the materials and tools we use are available via mail order or from on-line sources; see our list of suppliers on page 155.

We find the following items essentials:

- Turntable—Similar to a lazy Susan, the turntable makes finishing a cake more efficient. I use a heavy-duty metal turntable, but less expensive plastic versions will do the job.

- Cardboard rounds—These give stability to your cake, making it easy to handle and providing a clean edge to work with. You can purchase precut rounds in a variety of standard sizes, and if you will be making cakes often this is a worthwhile purchase. If you can't get your hands on the size you need, trace your cake pan onto a sheet of corrugated cardboard and cut the rounds out with a matte knife.

- Serrated knife—Also used for cutting bread, these wavy-edged blades are best for cutting and carving cakes. I recommend one 12 inches or longer.

- Metal spatula—Metal spatulas come in a variety of shapes and sizes. Their function is to spread and smooth icings and fillings. I use a 12-inch offset spatula and a smaller "baby bent" most, but find which is comfortable for you and that you can control easily.

- Metal scraper—A flat, stainless-steel metal scraper is useful for giving your cake a smooth finish. It performs the same task as a metal spatula but it is more rigid and makes icing a cake with a variegated finish a breeze.

- Rubber spatula—We use tons of rubber spatulas at the Bakehouse. They are perfect for mixing colors into icing or chocolate, as well as for folding ingredients into cake batters.

- Pastry bag—These cone-shaped bags make piping a whiz. When you use them in conjunction with a coupler (see below), you can go from piping lines to roses with one quick change of a tip. For buttercream choose a 12-inch or 14-inch polyester bag, which can be washed and reused.

- Coupler and ring—A plastic coupler that fits inside your pastry bag makes it possible to change tips easily when piping buttercream. A tip is placed over the end of the bag and the ring screws on top to secure the tip in place.

- Parchment paper—This versatile paper is similar to wax paper

without the meltable wax coating. Use it to line cookie sheets or cake pans to prevent baked goods from sticking. Chocolate doesn't stick to it either, so any chocolate design, no matter how delicate, can be piped onto it without losing any details when it is flipped.

You can also use parchment to make paper pastry cones for piping small amounts of colored butter-creams or chocolate. To make parchment cones, cut a 10-inch square diagonally in half to form two right triangles. With the 90-degree angle facing you, hold the two opposite corners and curl them toward the right angle. Overlapping one side over the other, pull one point around until it lines up with the other. Fold the points in, and tape close to the base to hold the cone's shape.

• Disposable pastry bags—If you do not want to make your own pastry cones, disposable plastic pastry bags can be used for piping with chocolate. They can be microwaved if the chocolate starts to harden.

• Cellophane—At the Bakehouse we buy 10 × 10-inch squares of cellophane in bulk, but cellophane also comes on rolls. I make all of my pastry cones from cellophane because it holds up well in the microwave and maintains

a clean, sharp point as you work. Cut the cellophane into 10-inch squares, or 5 × 10-inch rectangles. Hold the far right corner between your middle and index fingers and turn your hand toward the center; a point should begin to form at the center line. Continue this motion while wrapping the far left point around, pulling up on the far left point to form a sharp point at the tip of the cone. Tape close to the base to maintain the cone shape.

Cellophane, when cut into 2 × 10-inch strips, is also indispensable for icing shaped or rounded cakes. Being flexible, it can smooth curves as a metal spatula can't. Pipe chocolate decorations on cellophane to give them sheen.

• Flower nail—Flower nails come in many shapes and sizes, depending on the flower you are going to make. I use a 2-inch-diameter flower nail for making roses as well as when I want to pipe out pansies or other flowers with more time and care.

• Tips (leaf, petal, star, flat, round)—There is a special tip for almost every piping application. For a good selection of tips, I recommend buying a starter set. With the exception of the rose and the chrysanthemum, every piping technique in this book can be made with a basic starter set.

• Paintbrush—A soft-bristled brush of sable or acrylic is best for painting with chocolate. If you want a more textured effect, use bristle brushes.

A paintbrush is also used to apply luster dust, either by brushing it on or by dipping and blowing on the brush to give the cake an allover iridescent sheen.

- Dowels—Wooden dowels are necessary to support tiered cakes; without them, the cakes would collapse from the weight of the top tiers. I use dowels ⅛ inch to ¼ inch in diameter depending on the size of the cake; they are available at hardware and craft stores. Cut them with pruning sheers. For small-tiered cakes, drinking straws can be substituted.

Edible Supplies:

- Wafer chocolate—Wafer chocolate is actually not chocolate, it is a candy coating also known as confectioners' chocolate. It is easier to work with than chocolate because it does not need to be tempered and it has a lower melting point. It comes in dark chocolate, white chocolate, and a limited range of premixed colors.

- Liquid gel colors—For achieving the most vividly hued buttercreams, we depend on this professional product, which is sold at most high-end baking supply stores or through mail order. However, for butter-creams made with regular shortening rather than the shortening with an advanced emulsifier we use at the Bakehouse (see below), liquid-gel colors tend not to blend completely. Paste colors work nearly as well and are more readily available, but we recommend using candy colors (see below), if you do not want the color to form separated beads.

- Candy colors—These oil-based colors are used by confectioners to tint white chocolate; find them at candy-making specialty stores, at craft stores, or from mail-order sources. I also find they work well for coloring buttercream.

- High-ratio shortening—A specialty product for bakers, high-ratio shortening contains emulsifiers that allow it to remain stable at a wider range of temperatures and enable it to hold more air when beaten, making icings fluffier. It can also incorporate more sugar and liquid than regular shortening can without breaking, and it accepts coloring agents better. If you cannot get this product, however, regular shortening will give you fine results.

Fun Extras:

- Edible glitter—To give your cake a bit of glistening fairy dust.

- Luster dusts—These edible metallic powders give your cakes and designs an iridescent glow.

- Sprinkles/nonpareils—These little beads of color are perfect for cupcakes and kids' cakes.

- Dragées—Used sparingly, these hard, round metallic candies add sophisticated sparkle.

Working with Chocolate

Except for piped buttercream applications like roses, all the cake ornaments in this book are made from chocolate that has been melted, formed into a design, and then hardened again. I use confectioners' chocolate, which differs from "real" chocolate in that it contains vegetable oil rather than cocoa oil. It doesn't require tempering and can be melted and remelted as needed, making it much easier to work with. Confectioners' chocolate is also known as candy coating, but throughout the book I refer to it as wafer chocolate because it is most commonly sold in disk form, either in white or dark chocolate or premixed colors.

Even though it is much more forgiving than regular chocolate, there are some tricks to working with wafer chocolate. Chocolate is sensitive to weather changes, so store it in a cool, dry place. I have learned the hard way that when making chocolate designs it is important to work in a room where the temperature does not deviate much from 72°F. When the room is too cool the chocolate hardens too quickly and may warp; too warm and the chocolate doesn't set properly, so that details melt into the form itself. The chocolate may also get clumpy and hard to work with.

Here are some tips for working with chocolate:

- Do not get any water in the chocolate, as this will cause it to "seize." Seizing is when chocolate resolidifies and becomes lumpy. To counteract any seizing that may occur on humid days, try whisking in a few drops of vegetable oil.

- Because water makes chocolate seize, don't use liquid gel colors to tint chocolate; instead, use oil-based candy colors.

- I recommend melting chocolate in the microwave in a small glass or plastic bowl, but you can also melt the chocolate over a double boiler. Chocolate burns easily, so be careful. It is important that the melted chocolate be at body temperature (about 100°F.) and no hotter. When it

is overheated, chocolate will become solid, and unworkable. Microwave the chocolate in 30-second intervals, stirring in between, to ensure the chocolate does not burn; it will take approximately 1½ minutes to melt 1 cup of chocolate, but times will vary based on the room temperature, the amount of chocolate being melted, and the power of your microwave. Stirring the chocolate vigorously will often melt any remaining small pieces.

- To facilitate the decorating process in a cool environment, have all of your chocolate melted before you begin a design.

- Finished chocolate designs can be stored for at least a week and up to a month or more in a cool place in an airtight container. Never store chocolate designs in the freezer.

Color

Anyone who has seen a case full of finished cakes at Riviera Bakehouse knows I love color. The palette I choose changes every day according to my mood, the occasion for which the cake is intended, the season, and the weather, and so should yours; decide for yourself what colors should be mixed for a particular design depending on your whim or desire. Experiment; after all, innovations often result from unintentional discoveries.

That said, I generally decide on an overall palette for a cake before I start mixing the colors. Is the effect to be warm or cool, vibrant or subdued? I like to think about colors in terms of sun and shade: Oranges and reds are bright and hot like the sun, while blues and purples are cool and soft, like shade. However, every color has its warm and cool side. Lime green is hot while mint green is cool. Similarly, many warm colors when diluted with white create soothing sherbet colors. In general, warm colors predominate in the summer and fall, while cool colors predominate in the winter and spring.

I tend to use a bright or neon palette for more playful cakes; earthy or muted tones make for a more formal, subdued cake. This is not a hard-and-fast rule, though. Complementary colors like hot orange-yellow and cool lilac look beautiful together when a variety of yellows and purples are added to bridge the contrast.

Combining warm with subdued or cool with whimsical also adds interest to a palette. For example, the autumnal palette of burnt orange, burgundy, ocher, and plum is both warm and muted. A cake for a baby shower is an occasion for pumping traditional pastels up a notch, the lively palette reflecting a joyous time.

To get the vivid colors that are the hallmark of the Bakehouse, I color my buttercream and white wafer chocolate designs with specifically formulated products that are widely available at gourmet and bakeware supply stores, or from a variety of mail-order sources (see page 155 for more information).

For coloring buttercream my preference is liquid gel colors, a hybrid of liquid and paste colors that yields rich hues, though you can also use either liquids or pastes themselves. A basic palette needs only the primary colors: red, yellow, and blue. These three colors can be combined in a variety of ways to mix basic secondary and tertiary colors. To create a truly rich and dynamic palette, however, you will need more colors. I recommend a starting palette of yellow, red, royal blue, leaf green, violet, brown, and neon pink, which can be supplemented later for greater versatility; I find burgundy, orange, flesh tone, teal green, and sky blue indispensable.

For coloring white wafer chocolate I use candy colors. These oil-based colors tint chocolate without causing it to seize as the water-based liquid gel colors would, and their formulation allows them to combine perfectly with the chocolate, which is also oil-based. Powdered colors can be used instead, but the colors will not be as rich or vibrant, and the powder does not always dissolve completely. Wafer chocolates also come premixed in a limited though useful range of colors.

You may also use candy colors to tint your buttercreams if you find that liquid gel colors are not dissolving fully. They come in a far more limited range of colors—generally only yellow, orange, red, blue, green, violet, pink, and black—but if you want to limit your investment as you try your hand at working with chocolate and tint buttercream as well, the candy colors are the most versatile product.

COLOR MIXING CHART

The colors below are mixed from a palette of red, royal blue, leaf green, yellow, orange, neon pink, violet, sky blue, teal, burgundy, and brown. You can mix burgundy, teal, and sky blue yourself if you prefer not to buy many colors to start, but they will not be as pure. Candy color is not available in brown; for those formulas, use melted dark wafer chocolate in place of brown coloring. You may not be able to mix a true sky blue or teal, depending on the range of colors available in the brand you buy; if these colors are important for your designs, I recommend buying a bag of premixed wafer chocolate.

Use this chart as an approximate guide for mixing colors. Your results may vary depending on the brand of coloring you use, as they do vary in intensity. These formulas are based on drops of liquid-gel colors per ¼ cup of House Buttercream and drops of candy colors per ¼ cup of melted white wafer chocolate.

COLOR	BUTTERCREAM with liquid gel colors	WAFER CHOCOLATE with candy colors
red	5 red	10 red
pale pink	½ pink	½ pink
muted pink	1 pink + ½ brown	1 pink + 4 chocolate
neon pink	4 pink	5 pink
burgundy	5 burgundy	5 red + 2 purple + 2 pink
watermelon-red	3 red + 3 pink	5 red + 3 pink
pink-purple (fuchsia)	2 purple + 3 pink	1½ purple + 1½ pink
mauve	1 burgundy or ½ purple + ½ pink	½ purple + ½ pink
lilac	1 purple	1 pink + 4 chocolate
purple	3 purple	4 purple
ice blue	1 blue	1 blue
sky blue	3 sky blue	3 blue
royal blue	5 blue	6 blue
midnight blue	5 blue + 4 purple	5 blue + 3 purple
periwinkle	1 blue + 1 purple	1 blue + 1 purple
light lime	½ green + ½ yellow	½ green + ½ yellow

COLOR	BUTTERCREAM with liquid gel colors	WAFER CHOCOLATE with candy colors
lime green	2 green + 4 yellow	3 green + 7 yellow
sage green	2 green + 1 brown	4 green + 25 chocolate
leaf green	4 green + 1 blue + 1 brown	4 green + 10 chocolate + 1 blue + 1 yellow
teal green	4 teal or 1 green + 1 blue	3 blue + 1 green
mint green	1 green	1 green
blue-green	2 green + 2 blue	5 green + 2 blue
yellow-green	1 green + 3 yellow	1 green + 3 yellow
autumn green	3 green + 1 orange + 1 yellow + 1 brown	3 green + 1 yellow + 1 orange + 5 chocolate
yellow	1 yellow	4 yellow
soft yellow	1 yellow + ½ orange	1 yellow
yellow-orange	2 yellow + 1 orange or 2 yellow + 3 orange	5 yellow + 2 orange or 5 yellow + 4 orange
peach	1 orange	1 orange
salmon	1 pink + 1 orange	2 orange + 1pink
orange	3 orange	4 orange
red-orange	3 red + 4 orange	5 orange + 3 red
brown	4 brown	chocolate
burnt sienna	3 brown + 3 orange + 1 red	7 orange + 4 red + 18 chocolate

The Basics of Cake Assembly

Assembling a cake is a three-part process: filling, crumbing, and icing. These steps and the order in which they are performed never vary. With the exception of the truffle cake and cheesecakes, they are the first steps for every single cake in the pages that follow.

This is not to say you don't have options. Depending on the kind of celebration the cake is intended for—be it solemn, silly, or somewhere in between —you may want your cake to be lofty and level or tilted to a jaunty angle. Would a simple single layer do the trick or is an elaborate multitiered cake called for? Should it be iced in colorful buttercream or a sleek chocolate glaze?

For simplicity's sake we will assume you are baking a single-tiered, 9-inch round cake with three layers for which you will bake two 9-inch round cakes, one of which will be split to create the bottom and top layers. However, the process is exactly the same for a cake of any size and any number of tiers (see page 119 for more information on assembling multitiered cakes).

Here are a few hints to ensure good results:

- Never work with a warm cake, because it will crumble easily. Chilling the cake in the refrigerator for a few hours or overnight makes it much easier to work with. You can also wrap the cooled cake tightly in plastic wrap and freeze it for up to 2 weeks, letting it thaw when you're ready to use it.

- To ensure that the cake is stable, your fillings should be as stiff as possible. If you are using one of our flavored whipped cream mousses, make sure the cream is whipped to very stiff peaks before you add the flavorings; otherwise the filling will be too soft to work with and may ooze out the sides. Whipped cream fillings that sit too long will eventually break down, so prepare the filling just before you fill the cake.

- In nearly every case you should use the same icing to crumb the cake that you will use to finish it. There are two exceptions to this rule: Any cake finished with a color should be crumbed with uncolored buttercream, so don't tint your buttercream until you are ready to apply the finishing touches. Cakes that get a coating of Chocolate Glaze (page 39) should be crumbed with Whipped Chocolate Ganache (page 60) or Chocolate Buttercream (page 38) because they are more stable than mousses.

- Buttercream is the most stable of our icings. It holds up well under most weather conditions and acts as a protective shell, keeping the cake and filling fresh. For the fullest flavor, we recommend serving all cakes at room temperature. Keep in mind, the larger the cake, the longer it will take to get to room temperature. In warmer weather, it will take less time for your cake to reach room temperature, but cakes iced in buttercream, as long as they are not in direct sunlight, can still be taken out of the refrigerator hours before serving. In cold weather you can leave a cake out anywhere from 3 hours to all day. Once a cake has come to room temperature do not move it, however, because the layers may shift, and the design might break.

- Every cake needs a base from which to serve it. This base should be strong enough to support the cake if you must move it, and it should be at least 2 inches larger in diameter than the cake itself; this will give you space for borders and/or designs around the bottom. Cake plates and footed stands look great, but they're not a good choice if you will be traveling with the cake, as the cake may slide off. To make a simple base, glue a doily to a cardboard round of the same size. Cardboard rounds can also be covered with foil; double or triple the cardboards for a stronger base. For tiered cakes we recommend a solid, inflexible base like ½-inch-thick wood or Plexiglas. Cover it with foil or grease-resistant fabric, or leave it as is for a rustic appeal. In most cases you can simply glue the cardboard round supporting the cake to your chosen base. I don't recommend gluing your cardboard round to a cake plate or stand; instead use a dab of buttercream or icing to secure it in place.

What you will need:

- cardboard round exactly the same diameter as the cake
- cake plate or foil-covered cardboard round at least 2 inches larger than the cake, for a base
- serrated knife
- metal spatula; optional, metal scraper

- pastry bag with coupler
- turntable

In addition, for glazed cakes:

- Sheet pan
- Wire cooling rack
- Chocolate shavings or chocolate sprinkles (optional)

FILLING

The first step to assembling your baked and cooled cakes is splitting and filling the layers. Because we use a wide variety of fillings, which range in density, the method described below will ensure that the layers remain level and in place. You will need approximately 4 cups of filling and 4 cups of icing to fill, crumb, and finish a 9-inch cake.

1. Start by leveling the layers. Most cakes form a rounded dome when they are baked, so you will need to level the tops. Use a serrated knife and, keeping the knife horizontal, use a sawing action to cut off the rounded portions. If the bottom of the cake has baked dark, trim a thin layer off of there, too.

2. Cut the cakes into additional layers. If you have baked two cakes, cut the thicker one in half horizontally. (For cakes baked in one layer, cut three equal layers.) To cut even layers, place the cake on a turntable. Rotate the turntable, lightly scoring the cake with a serrated knife at the place where it is to be cut in halves or thirds. Make sure the cut line is level and divides the cake equally. With your hand lightly resting on the cake to hold it steady, rotate the turntable as you use a sawing action to cut the cake along the guideline. You should now have 3 layers.

3. Stack all 3 layers in the center of the cardboard round with the thickest one, usually the unsplit cake, in the center of the stack. Adhere the bottom layer to the cardboard with a drop of buttercream if you like. If the cake protrudes over the cardboard, trim the sides, but it should be no more than ¼ inch from the cardboard edge.

4. Fill a pastry bag, with a coupler inside, with buttercream. Carefully set aside the top two layers. You can slide a cardboard round under the layers for stability when moving. Pipe a ring of buttercream around the edge of the bottom layer. This will create a reservoir to contain the filling and prevent it from oozing into your final covering. The ring should be as tall as the coupler is wide; if the ring is too short, pipe another ring on top of the first to create a sufficiently high border.

5. Fill the reservoir you've created with half of the filling and spread it level with the ring. Don't allow the filling to extend above the border.

6. Place the second layer of cake on top of the first, making sure it is centered and level. Ring and fill the second layer as above.

7. Center the third layer on top of the first two. Press gently with your hand to level the cake.

Note that if the filling of the cake is the same as the icing you do not need to ring the cake (i.e., Whipped Cream Filling with Whipped Cream Icing, Whipped Chocolate Ganache with Chocolate Glaze, Cream Cheese Filling with Cream Cheese Icing, or buttercream filling with buttercream icing).

CRUMBING

Just as an artist primes her canvas before beginning to paint, you must pre-pare the surface of your filled cake for further decoration. Applying a thin coat-ing of icing over the entire cake will seal in the crumbs and create a smooth backdrop for piped, spread, and applied decorations. Once chilled, this layer will also prevent crumbs from appearing in your final coat.

1. Place the filled cake in the center of the turntable.

2. Place a small amount of icing on top of the cake. With a metal spatula, spread the icing evenly over the entire top of the cake, making it as smooth as possible. Use the excess icing that comes over the edge to cover the sides. If necessary add more icing to cover the sides of the cake with a smooth coat. You will need approximately 1 cup of icing to crumb a 9-inch cake. The icing can go up to but not over the cardboard round.

3. Chill the cake. Cakes crumbed in butter-cream should be refrigerated for at least 15 minutes or until the cake has set. Cakes crumbed with whipped cream or Whipped Chocolate Ganache should be placed in the freezer until set. (Do not remove cakes crumbed with Whipped Chocolate Ganache until you are ready to glaze them with Chocolate Glaze.)

FILLING A TILTED CAKE

Tilting its layers at a rakish angle gives a cake a playful quality that is perfect for birthdays or celebration cakes. When customers see our tilted cakes they often assume they were baked that way or that we trim the cakes on a slant; in fact, we create the tilt with the filling. You can use almost any filling, but we recommend those that are stiff and hold their form well, such as Whipped Cream, Cookies and Cream, Cinnamon Whipped Cream, Whipped Chocolate Ganache, Raspberry Mousse, Chocolate Hazelnut Mousse, or Coffee Mousse. Orange Mousse, Lemon Mousse, and French Custard are slightly less stable and therefore less practical choices.

1. Start by leveling the layers as described on page 30. Cut the cake into additional layers as needed.

2. Stack the cake layers on the cardboard round, adhering the bottom layer with a drop of buttercream. Trim the sides of the cake if it protrudes over the cardboard.

3. Pipe a ring around the edge of the first layer. The ring should be as high as the coupler is wide. Fill the reservoir created with one third of the filling and spread it evenly, keeping it within the ring to prevent seepage or instability.

4. Center the second layer on top. Ring the second layer once around the entire circumference, then make a second half ring on top of the first. Add another half ring if needed to make the cake tilt. Spread the remaining two thirds of the filling in the reservoir, using the top of the ring as a guideline. There should be a decided slope.

5. Center the third layer on top of the filling. Press gently with your hand to even the angle.

6. Crumb coat and finish as you would a level cake.

ICING THE CAKE

Now comes the creative part, the part that helps set the mood of your occasion, be it a colorful fiesta or a sophisticated evening. This is also the step that requires the most decisions and the most finesse.

You may decide simply to ice the top of the cake, putting only enough icing on the sides to help coatings like chocolate shavings, crumbs, nuts, or shredded coconut adhere. For more refined embellishments like piping and appliquéd chocolate decorations, the smooth finish achieved with a final coating of butter-cream or chocolate glaze is best. Whipped cream icing, though delicious, is not stiff enough to support decorations, so if you choose it, finish the sides with one of the coatings mentioned above or just serve it plain.

With Buttercream

Buttercream mixes well with color and it provides the ideal backdrop for a design. To soften the buttercream slightly to make it easier to spread smoothly, heat it gently in the top of a double boiler over simmering water, stirring often, until it is soft and spreadable. Your final coat of buttercream should be thin—just thick enough to cover the crumb coat.

1. Prepare the icing for the final coat, coloring your buttercream as desired. Place the cake in the center of the turntable.

2. With a metal spatula, spread a small amount of icing (approximately ½ cup for a 9-inch cake) evenly over the top of the cake.

3. Ice the sides of the cake, using about 2 cups of buttercream. Load the spatula with icing and run the bottom edge of the spatula along the contour of the cardboard, being careful to keep the spatula upright. Hold the spatula perpendicular to and flush against the cardboard to ensure even distribution of the icing. Reload the spatula as needed until the sides are covered.

4. Smooth the sides by holding the spatula upright against the side of cake. Slowly spin the turntable without lifting the spatula from the cake's surface. Remove any excess buttercream with the spatula. This step is probably the

most challenging to master. I find it helpful to have a container of hot water nearby to dip my spatula in (dry it off afterward). The heat will melt the buttercream, giving it a smooth surface.

5. A lip of excess buttercream will have formed at the top edge of the cake. Use your spatula to gently sweep the excess buttercream toward the center around the entire circumference of the cake until the top is smooth and level.

6. Adhere the cake's cardboard base to a cake plate or other base. If the base is disposable or you are going to be traveling with the cake, use glue; otherwise place the cake on the base you will be serving from.

7. Chill the cake until one to four hours before serving, depending on the temperature.

With Chocolate Glaze

Unlike buttercream, which takes practice to get smooth, chocolate glaze pours over the prepared cake surface, hiding most imperfections without much effort. Because it is easy to work with, delicious, and beautiful, this is my favorite choice for icing a cake.

1. Work with the chocolate glaze at body temperature (approximately 100°F.). If you premade the glaze, gently reheat it in the top of a double boiler. Be careful not to overheat the glaze or it will lose its shine, crack when dry, or cause the crumb coat to melt.

2. Place a cooling rack on a sheet pan and place the filled, trimmed cake on the rack.

3. Pour or ladle the glaze around the top edge of the cake, allowing the glaze to run down the sides. Pour the remaining glaze on top. Immediately run a metal spatula over the top of the glaze to push the excess over the sides, being careful not to touch the cake itself. Make sure the sides are covered completely. Shake the sheet pan lightly to help the glaze settle.

4. If you like, press chocolate shavings or chocolate sprinkles onto the sides of the cake.

5. Adhere the cake's cardboard base to a cake plate or other base. If the base is disposable or you are going to be traveling with the cake, use glue; otherwise place the cake on the base you will be serving from.

6. Chill the cake until one to four hours before serving, depending on the temperature.

Basic Icings

These are the icing recipes we use again and again at the Bakehouse; almost every recipe in this book is made using one of these three. We've also included a quick-and-easy whipped cream icing for those times when you just want a pretty, tasty finish without a lot of effort.

HOUSE BUTTERCREAM

We inherited the recipe for House Buttercream from the previous owner of the Bakehouse and decided to keep it, as it has been used in some of the bakery's most beloved cakes for more than forty years. It is a pure white buttercream that is ideal for mixing with colors, from fluorescent pink to muted green. Because it contains some shortening in addition to butter, it has a lighter flavor that some people prefer to the richness of Kaye's decadent all-butter buttercream. We use high-ratio shortening, which can be found at any good cake-decorating supply store; it does not affect the taste, but it does affect the buttercream's ability to accept color. If you can't find high-ratio shortening, substitute regular vegetable shortening, but use candy colors to tint your buttercream to avoid tiny beads of unblended color.

House Buttercream can be stored in the refrigerator for up to 2 weeks if tightly covered.

In the bowl of an electric mixer, stir together:

>   **6 cups confectioners' sugar**
>
>   **½ teaspoon salt**
>
>   **1 teaspoon vanilla extract**

With a whisk attachment, add and whip at low speed:

>   **1 cup boiling water (¾ cup on hot days)**

Whip until smooth and cool.

Add and whip until smooth:

>   **2¾ cups high-ratio or regular vegetable shortening**
>
>   **6 ounces (1½ sticks) slightly chilled butter, cut into 1-inch pieces**

Increase the speed to medium-high. Whip until light, fluffy, and doubled in volume (10 to 20 minutes).

The buttercream will almost fill a 5-quart mixing bowl.

Yield: 9½ cups

KAYE'S BUTTERCREAM

People who think they do not like buttercream have probably never had the real thing. I think my Italian meringue buttercream is just the best. It is stable enough to hold up for those summer wedding cakes; it keeps well; it has a silky-smooth texture; and it mixes beautifully with flavors like chocolate, espresso, raspberry, lemon, or hazelnut. We use 40 to 60 gallons a week at the Bakehouse. Any leftover buttercream should be stored in the refrigerator and will stay fresh for up to 2 weeks. To use the chilled buttercream, bring it to room temperature and beat at medium speed in the bowl of an electric mixer until smooth and creamy. To speed up this process you can lightly reheat the buttercream over hot water before beating. Tinting the buttercream will not produce colors quite as bright or pure as the House Buttercream because the butter content imparts a subtle yellow cast.

In a saucepan, bring to a boil:

½ cup water

2¼ cups sugar

Use a clean brush and cold water to wash down any sugar crystals that form on the sides of the pan as the water heats. When the sugar comes to a boil set a timer for 7 minutes, and let boil.

After 5 minutes, in the bowl of an electric mixer, begin to whip at high speed:

1 cup egg whites (about 12 large egg whites)

Whip until stiff. They should be done when the timer goes off.

With the mixer on high speed, slowly beat the sugar syrup into the egg whites, pouring the syrup to the side of the bowl to avoid the whip.

Continue to beat until the bowl is cool to the touch, about 10 minutes. Slowly add:

1½ pounds (6 sticks) unsalted butter at room temperature, cut into 1-inch pieces

When the buttercream begins to jump out of the bowl, reduce the speed to low.

Mix in at low speed:

1 teaspoon pure vanilla extract

Beat until light and fluffy. At some points the mixture might look curdled. Just keep beating; it will become smooth again.

Yield: 8 cups

(continued on next page)

Variations The luxurious flavor of buttercream is even more sumptuous with the addition of chocolate or raspberry. Tart or slightly bitter flavors, like lemon curd or espresso powder, take the sweet edge off of plain vanilla buttercream for a very sophisticated flavor.

CHOCOLATE BUTTERCREAM

Stir in 2 to 3 ounces of melted, body-temperature (100°F.) semisweet chocolate per 1 cup of Kaye's Buttercream. Mix until smooth and completely blended, scraping down the sides of the bowl to prevent the chocolate from hardening and causing unmelted flecks in the buttercream.

LEMON BUTTERCREAM

Stir in ¼ cup lemon curd per 2 cups of Kaye's Buttercream. Mix until smooth and completely blended.

RASPBERRY BUTTERCREAM

Stir in ¼ cup (or to taste and color) raspberry purée per 2 cups of Kaye's Buttercream. Mix until smooth and completely blended.

CHOCOLATE HAZELNUT BUTTERCREAM

Stir in ¼ cup (or to taste and color) chocolate hazelnut spread per 1½ cups of Kaye's Buttercream. Mix until smooth and completely blended.

COFFEE BUTTERCREAM

In a bowl, dissolve 2 tablespoons instant espresso powder in 2 tablespoons of hot water. Whisk in 3 cups of Kaye's Buttercream. Mix until smooth and completely blended.

CHOCOLATE GLAZE

This basic recipe for chocolate glaze icing comes from Luiz Silva, my much-loved son-in-law, but I added a little more cream to make it easier to work with. It is a delicious, easy, and elegant covering for almost any cake. With the addition of 2 cups of hot cream and ¼ cup of Grand Marnier, it makes a fabulous dessert sauce for ice cream or plated desserts.

In a metal bowl over hot water, melt:

> **3 pounds semisweet chocolate, cut into small pieces**

In a saucepan, warm over medium-high heat:

> **1 quart heavy cream**
>
> **10 ounces (2½ sticks) unsalted butter**
>
> **½ cup light corn syrup**

Stir until the butter melts, then continue to heat to just before the boiling point. Slowly pour the scalded liquid over the melted chocolate, whisking constantly until smooth. Strain the icing through a fine sieve. The icing can be used immediately or cooled and refrigerated for up to 2 weeks. If it has been chilled, reheat slowly in a double boiler before using.

Yield: 11 cups

WHIPPED CREAM

Whipped cream is a light alternative to buttercream and a perfect accompaniment for fruit filling or chocolate cake. Because whipped cream breaks down easily, it is not a stable foundation for a design; however, if you are going for taste over appearance or want to make an undecorated cake or just apply decorations to the top or perhaps some crumbs or sprinkles around the sides, go with whipped cream.

In the bowl of an electric mixer, whip until stiff:

> **3 cups heavy whipping cream**
>
> **4 tablespoons confectioners' sugar, sifted**
>
> **1 teaspoon vanilla extract**

Yield: 6 cups

part two
SIMPLE CAKES

Now that we have covered the basics, it's time to move on to more creative ventures. Here are eleven cakes to get you started decorating. Each cake illustrates a different decorating technique, starting with some that are very easy to master and introducing techniques that may take a bit more practice to get the hang of. Do note, however, that you can simplify any cake by eliminating some of the details and embellishments, or by using fewer colors.

Many of these designs use melted colored chocolate. In general, I have listed generous chocolate amounts to make it easier to mix colors. You may want to limit the number of colors you use if you are just making one or two small designs. For instance, the snowman on page 96 requires only ½ cup of chocolate in total but has decorations in several colors. In such instances you have a couple of choices: You can limit the number of colors you use for surface embellishments (our dapper snowman will look just as fashionable with two colors instead of eight), or you can make multiple motifs and either use them to further decorate the cake or store them for a future use (remembering, of course, that chocolate should never be stored in the freezer or refrigerator).

We have suggested cakes, fillings, and icings that we feel suit the mood of each design. For instance, the Sunflower Cake is made with either Golden Butter Cake or Orange Butter Cake, both of which have a yellow color reminiscent of the sun. The cake is filled with Orange Mousse for a light and summery accent. These combinations are certainly not set in stone; feel free to mix and match flavors to customize your cake. To make the cakes larger or smaller, simply refer to the Baking Times and Cake Assemblage charts (pages 157 and 156) to calculate the amounts of cake, filling, and icing you will need.

Ode to Jackson Pollock

Making this cake is like scribbling on a big pad of paper. Let go of any inhibitions you might have about decorating cakes and enjoy this abstract expressionist experience. It is easy and fun, and the end result is raw beauty. This technique can be applied to any glazed cake.

What you will need:

Cake: one 10-inch round cake of your choice (we recommend the Mocha Chocolate Chip Cheesecake, Grand Marnier Cheesecake, or Julie's Chocolate Peanut Butter Swirl Cheesecake, pages 46, 44, and 48)

Icing: Chocolate Glaze (page 39)

1 cup each dark wafer chocolate and white wafer chocolate

1 cup chocolate shavings or chocolate sprinkles

How to:

1. Bake the cheesecake and let it cool completely. Unmold the cake onto a cardboard round and freeze until set, about 3 hours or overnight. Prepare the Chocolate Glaze.

2. Place the cake on a wire rack set inside a sheet pan. Glaze the cake as directed on page 35.

3. In small bowls, melt 1 cup each of white and dark wafer chocolate separately.

4. Dip a whisk or a fork in the white chocolate, then flick your wrist in the direction of the cake, directing the spatters over the top of the cake. Repeat a few times until you are satisfied with the pattern, then repeat the spattering process with the dark chocolate.

5. Lift the cake from the rack and carefully clean the bottom edge with a hot spatula. The hot spatula helps to melt any chocolate that might have stuck to the cooling rack. Press chocolate shavings or chocolate sprinkles around the bottom of the cake.

6. Adhere the cardboard round supporting the cake to your base.

GRAND MARNIER CHEESECAKE

When I was working as a pastry chef for a restaurant in Pearl River, New York, I had to make a different cheesecake every week. I was very proud of this Grand Marnier Cheesecake because it was one of the first recipes I developed myself. It has a light, silky-smooth texture with a soft orange flavor. Since cheesecakes freeze beautifully, try baking this recipe in three 7-inch pans. You will have one to eat, one to freeze, and one to give to a friend.

Orange Cookie Crust

Line a cookie sheet with parchment paper. Grease a 10 × 3-inch round cake pan and line it on the bottom with parchment paper. Have all ingredients at room temperature.

In the bowl of an electric mixer at medium speed, beat to combine:

> **8 ounces (2 sticks) unsalted butter**
>
> **¾ cup confectioners' sugar**

On a piece of wax paper, sift together:

> **1½ cups all-purpose flour**
>
> **¾ cup cornstarch**

Add to the butter mixture and mix at low speed until a soft dough forms.

Add and mix at low speed until well combined:

> **1 tablespoon grated orange zest**
>
> **1 teaspoon vanilla extract**

On a lightly floured board roll the dough into 2 logs. Wrap in plastic wrap or wax paper and chill for 2 to 3 hours or overnight.

Preheat the oven to 350°F. Slice the chilled dough into ¼-inch-thick rounds and arrange 1 inch apart on the cookie sheet. Bake for 12 to16 minutes, or until golden brown. Let cool on a wire rack.

In a food processor chop enough cookies to make:

> **2½ cups cookie crumbs**

Transfer the crumbs to a bowl and stir in:

> **2 ounces (½ stick) melted butter**

Pour the crumb crust into the pan. Press firmly onto the bottom and one-third of the way up the sides.

Filling

Preheat the oven to 350°F.

Have all ingredients at room temperature.

In the bowl of an electric mixer, beat at medium speed until smooth, scraping down the bowl often:

2½ pounds cream cheese

Gradually beat in:

1¼ cups sugar

When the sugar is combined, scrape the bowl again and add, at low speed:

¼ cup heavy cream

¼ cup strained fresh orange juice

2 tablespoons Grand Marnier

2 tablespoons finely chopped candied orange peel (see Note)

1 tablespoon grated orange zest

Mix well, scraping the bowl down often. When combined add one at a time:

5 large eggs

Beat only until the eggs are fully incorporated.

Pour the filling into the crust. Place the pan in a larger pan and fill the larger pan halfway with hot water. Bake for 60 to 75 minutes, or until lightly golden and set. Let the cheesecake sit at room temperature for 1 to 2 hours before unmolding. To remove the cheesecake from the pan, run a paring knife around the edge of the cake, close to the pan so as not to break the crust. Cover the top of the cheesecake with plastic wrap and place a cake round or flat plate on top. Invert the cake onto the plate. Slowly lift off the cake pan and peel off the parchment paper. Place another cake round or plate on top (actually the bottom of the cheesecake) and invert again. Carefully peel the plastic wrap off without pulling off the skin of the cheesecake.

Note: To make candied orange peel, with a peeler or a sharp knife cut the zest from 2 oranges in long strips. Blanch in boiling water for 1 minute. Drain. Bring 2 cups of water and 1 cup of sugar to a boil. Add the peel and simmer on low heat for 1 hour. Store the orange peel in its syrup in the refrigerator for up to 4 weeks.

MOCHA CHOCOLATE CHIP CHEESECAKE

A customer once said our Mocha Chocolate Chip Cheesecake was better than sex. Decadent and rich in espresso flavor, this is an irresistible treat. If you are feeling lazy, you can purchase a plain chocolate cookie for your crust. If, however, you do make the cookies, any leftovers are great as sandwich cookies filled with jam, melted chocolate, or ice cream.

Chocolate Cookie Crust

Line a cookie sheet with parchment paper. Grease a 10 × 3-inch round cake pan and line it on the bottom with parchment paper. Have all ingredients at room temperature.

In the bowl of an electric mixer at medium speed, beat to combine:

> **8 ounces (2 sticks) unsalted butter**
>
> **½ cup sugar**

Add at medium low and beat until well combined:

> **2 large eggs**
>
> **2 teaspoons pure vanilla extract**

On a piece of wax paper, sift together:

> **½ cup Dutch-process cocoa**
>
> **2 cups all-purpose flour**
>
> **a pinch of salt**

Add all at once to the butter mixture and mix at low speed until combined.

Chill for 10 minutes. On a lightly floured board roll the dough into 2 logs. Wrap in plastic wrap or wax paper and chill for 2 to 3 hours or overnight.

Preheat the oven to 350°F. Slice the chilled dough into ¼-inch-thick rounds and arrange 1 inch apart on the cookie sheet. Bake for 14 to 18 minutes, or until firm to the touch. Let cool on a wire rack.

In a food processor finely chop enough cookies to make:

> **3 cups cookie crumbs**

Transfer the crumbs to a bowl and add:

> **¼ cup plus 2 tablespoons sugar**

Add and mix:

> **4½ ounces (1 stick plus 1 tablespoon) melted unsalted butter**

Pour the crumb crust into the pan. Press firmly onto the bottom and one third of the way up the sides.

Filling

Preheat the oven to 350°F.

Have all ingredients at room temperature.

In the bowl of an electric mixer, beat at medium speed until smooth, scraping down the bowl often:

2½ pounds cream cheese

Gradually beat in at medium speed:

1½ cups sugar

Meanwhile, simmer in a saucepan:

½ cup heavy cream

Remove from the heat.

Add and stir to dissolve:

1 tablespoon plus 1 teaspoon instant espresso powder

1½ teaspoons pure vanilla extract

Add the heavy cream mixture to the cream cheese and beat on low to incorporate, scraping down as needed.

Add one at a time at low speed:

6 large eggs

Beat only until the eggs are fully incorporated. Pour the filling into the crust.

Scatter over the top of the filling:

1¼ cups mini semisweet chocolate chips

Carefully swirl the chips into the filling with a small knife.

Place the pan in a larger pan and fill the larger pan halfway with hot water. Bake for 60 to 75 minutes, or until lightly golden and set. Let the cheesecake sit at room temperature for 1 to 2 hours before unmolding. To remove the cheesecake from the pan, run a paring knife around the edge of the cake, close to the pan so as not to break the crust. Cover the top of the cheesecake with plastic wrap and place a cake round or flat plate on top. Invert the cake onto the plate. Slowly lift off the cake pan and peel off the parchment paper. Place another cake round or plate on top (actually the bottom of the cheesecake) and invert again. Carefully peel the plastic wrap off without pulling off the skin of the cheesecake.

JULIE'S CHOCOLATE PEANUT BUTTER SWIRL CHEESECAKE

One of the high school girls who worked at the Bakehouse said she thought a peanut butter chocolate cheesecake would be great. I came up with this recipe and named it for her. She was delighted with her namesake. The irresistible combination of peanut butter and chocolate is sinfully rich and delicious.

Peanut Butter Cookie Crust

Line a cookie sheet with parchment paper. Grease a 10 × 3-inch round cake pan and line it on the bottom with parchment paper. Have all ingredients at room temperature.

In the bowl of an electric mixer, beat at medium speed until light in color:

> **6 ounces (1½ sticks) unsalted butter**
>
> **½ cup dark brown sugar, packed**
>
> **½ cup granulated sugar**
>
> **1 cup chunky peanut butter**

Add at medium-low speed and mix well:

> **1 large egg**
>
> **½ teaspoon pure vanilla extract**

Combine on a piece of wax paper, then add to the butter mixture at low speed:

> **1½ cups flour**
>
> **½ teaspoon salt**
>
> **½ teaspoon baking soda**

Cover and chill for 10 minutes. On a lightly floured board roll the dough into 2 logs. Wrap in plastic wrap or wax paper and chill for 2 to 3 hours or overnight.

Preheat the oven to 350°F. Slice the chilled dough into ¼-inch-thick rounds and arrange 1 inch apart on the cookie sheet. Bake for 12 to 15 minutes, or until golden. Let cool on a wire rack.

In a food processor finely chop enough cookies to make:

> **3¼ cups crumbs**

Transfer the crumbs to a bowl. Add and mix:

> **3 ounces (¾ stick) melted unsalted butter**

Pour the crumb crust into the pan. Press firmly onto the bottom and one third of the way up the sides.

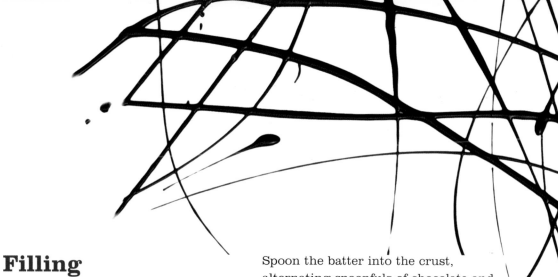

Filling

Preheat the oven to 350° F. Have all ingredients at room temperature.

In the bowl of an electric mixer, beat at medium speed until smooth, scraping down the bowl often:

2 pounds cream cheese

Add and mix well at medium speed:

1 cup chunky peanut butter

Gradually beat in:

1¼ cups sugar

Add and beat on low speed to incorporate, scraping down as needed:

½ cup heavy cream

1 teaspoon pure vanilla extract

Add one at a time:

5 large eggs

Beat only until the eggs are fully incorporated.

Transfer half the batter to a second bowl. To one half add:

8 ounces melted semisweet chocolate

Spoon the batter into the crust, alternating spoonfuls of chocolate and peanut butter. When you're done, swirl a small knife through the batter to make a decorative pattern on top.

Place the pan in a larger pan and fill the larger pan halfway with hot water. Bake for 60 to 75 minutes, or until lightly golden and set. Let the cheesecake sit at room temperature for 1 to 2 hours before unmolding. To remove the cheesecake from the pan, run a paring knife around the edge of the cake, close to the pan so as not to break the crust. Cover the top of the cheesecake with plastic wrap and place a cake round or flat plate on top. Invert the cake onto the plate. Slowly lift off the cake pan and peel off the parchment paper. Place another cake round or plate on top (actually the bottom of the cheesecake) and invert again. Carefully peel the plastic wrap off without pulling off the skin of the cheesecake.

Starry Night

Here is proof that even simple, one-color chocolate decorations against a clean glaze can make for a very distinctive cake. The shimmer of gold and silver is an elegant touch against the rich glaze and the sleek coating encloses a super-dense and delicious cake. Anything more elaborate would be overkill! For a more whimsical design, try coloring white chocolate to make yellow, orange, and lime-green stars.

What you will need:

Cake: one 9-inch round cake of your choice
(we recommend the Truffle Cake, page 53, or
the Chocolate Apricot Pecan Torte, page 52)

Icing: Chocolate Glaze (page 39)

Decoration: 1 cup dark wafer chocolate to make
8 to 10 chocolate stars

1 cup chocolate shavings or chocolate sprinkles

Silver and/or gold dragées

How to:

1. Bake the cake and let it cool completely. The Truffle Cake and Chocolate Apricot Pecan Torte do not need to be filled or crumb coated. Freeze until set, about 3 hours or overnight. Prepare the Chocolate Glaze.

2. Using the templates provided on page 54, pipe out 8 to 10 chocolate stars as illustrated in the One-Color Chocolate Method, page 54.

3. Glaze the cake as directed on page 35. Press chocolate shavings or chocolate sprinkles around the bottom of the cake.

4. Adhere the cardboard round supporting the cake to your base.

5. Before the glaze has set completely, arrange the stars on the top of the cake in an arc. Sprinkle dragées over the stars.

CHOCOLATE APRICOT PECAN TORTE

The Thanksgiving menu at the Bakehouse would not be complete without this cake. It is a dense, single-layer cake chock-full of pecans and macerated apricots. Don't worry if you have no rum on hand; brandy or even crème de cacao works just as well. Take care not to overbake and you will be rewarded with a moist cake reminiscent of a Chunky, a favorite candy bar from my childhood.

Grease and flour one 9 × 3-inch round pan and line the bottom with parchment paper. Preheat the oven to 350°F. Have all ingredients at room temperature.

In a bowl, combine and let stand for 1 hour or overnight:

> ⅓ cup dark rum
>
> 1¼ cups dried apricots

Chop the apricots with the liquid medium fine in a food processor, and set aside.

In a food processor combine and finely chop:

> 1½ cups pecans
>
> 1 tablespoon flour

In the bowl of an electric mixer at high speed, use the paddle attachment to cream together until light and fluffy:

> 6 ounces (1½ sticks) unsalted butter
>
> 1 cup sugar

Beat in one at a time at medium speed:

> 5 large eggs

The mixture may look curdled.

Add at low speed:

> 6 ounces semisweet chocolate, melted and cooled
>
> 1½ teaspoons pure vanilla extract

Add the chopped pecans and:

> ⅔ cup graham crackers crumbs (approximately 12 crackers)

When the mixture is blended, fold in the apricots.

Pour the batter into the pan. Bake 45 to 50 minutes, or until a cake tester inserted in the center has moist crumbs on it. Place on a wire rack and let cool completely before unmolding.

TRUFFLE CAKE

Every bakery worth its salt has its own version of this traditional bittersweet, dense cake. Here is ours. It sells well year-round, but we can't make enough for Passover because not only is it decadently rich, it is also flourless. Truffle cake, when eaten while still warm, has a silky-smooth, almost light texture very different than after it has been chilled. Either way it is sumptuous.

Grease and flour one 9 × 2-inch round pan and line the bottom with parchment paper.

Preheat the oven to 350°F.

Combine in a heatproof bowl placed over hot water:

>   8 ounces (2 sticks) unsalted butter
>
>   6 ounces semisweet chocolate
>
>   6 ounces unsweetened chocolate

Stir until melted, then cool 5 to 10 minutes.

In the bowl of an electric mixer at high speed, use a whisk attachment to beat:

>   5 large eggs
>
>   ½ cup sugar
>
>   2 teaspoons pure vanilla extract

Continue beating until triple in volume and the batter forms a ribbon when the beaters are lifted.

Meanwhile in a saucepan, heat to a full boil:

>   ½ cup sugar
>
>   ⅓ cup light corn syrup

Remove from the heat and slowly beat the hot syrup into the eggs with the mixer at low speed. Beat at medium speed until the batter reaches the top of the bowl, about 8 minutes, then decrease the speed to low and beat in half of the chocolate mixture. Before it is fully incorporated take off the whisk attachment and fold in the remaining chocolate by hand.

Pour the batter into the pan. Place the pan in a larger pan and fill the larger pan halfway with hot water. Bake for 40 minutes. The cake will look set. Cool the cake on a wire rack for 15 to 20 minutes, then turn it out of the pan onto a cake round. Cool completely, then chill before glazing.

Serve the cake at room temperature.

One-Color Chocolate Method

The first chocolate design I ever made was an axe that embellished our President's Day Lincoln Log. Since then I have made stars, hearts, polka dots, and even complex, detailed silhouettes. This is the easiest of the chocolate method designs. All you have to do is trace a form and fill it in; no shading or coloring is involved. The simplicity of the designs created with this technique belies its decorative potential.

Any template can be enlarged or reduced on a photocopy machine to fit the scale of your cake. I find it convenient to attach a long paper tab, or handle, to the template so I can easily slide it out from the parchment paper after piping my design, or move it to pipe out multiples without disrupting those I've already made.

What you will need:

Sheet pan

Parchment paper

1 to 2 cups dark wafer chocolate

Pastry cones

Soft-bristle paintbrush (such as sable or acrylic)

Silver and/or gold luster dust

How to:

1. Photocopy or trace the star template provided (at left) or draw your own with black marker. This will go beneath the parchment paper on which you pipe the chocolate to provide a guideline.

2. Place the template on a sheet pan or flat surface. Lay a sheet of parchment paper on top. Lightly secure the parchment paper with one or two pieces of tape.

3. Melt the chocolate. Pour the chocolate into a pastry cone and cut a small hole in the tip.

4. Trace the outline of the template with chocolate, then fill in. Alternatively, you can make a larger hole in the pastry cone, and simply fill in the area with large strokes without outlining first. The chocolate should be approximately ⅛ inch thick. Set the design aside to harden.

5. When it is dry, gently flip the design and carefully peel off the parchment paper.

6. With a paintbrush, dust the star lightly with iridescent silver or gold luster dust.

Fling

Originally named the Spring Fling, this design has become a year-round favorite with our customers. It's a simple design that can be altered to create many different effects. If you want a more tailored cake, try small white dots on a white icing or chocolate dots on Chocolate Glaze. This design works equally well with buttercream (see pages 60–61). You'll need 1 recipe of either Kaye's Buttercream (page 37) or House Buttercream (page 36) and a pastry bag and coupler with #104 and #102 petal tips for the ruffle borders around the bottom edge.

What you will need:

Cake: one 9-inch round cake of your choice (we recommend the Chocolate Chip Pound Cake, page 58, or the Lemon Ginger Cream Cheese Pound Cake, page 59)

Filling: Whipped Chocolate Ganache (page 60) for Chocolate Chip Pound Cake or Lemon Mousse (page 61) for Lemon Ginger Pound Cake

Icing: Chocolate Glaze (page 39)

Decoration: 1 to 2 cups white wafer chocolate to make 50 to 75 chocolate polka dots

Yellow, green, violet, pink, and/or blue candy color

1 to 2 cups white wafer chocolate

Chocolate shavings or chocolate sprinkles

How to:

1. Bake the cake and let it cool completely. Prepare the filling and icing. Fill and crumb coat the cake as directed on pages 30–32. Chill the filled cake.

2. Melt the wafer chocolate. Tint the chocolate with your choice of candy color. Pour the chocolate into a pastry cone and cut a medium-size hole.

3. On a sheet pan lined with parchment paper, pipe out approximately 50 polka dots. They can be uniform or varied in size, many colors or just one. Set aside to harden.

4. Prepare the chocolate glaze. Ice the cake.

5. Before the icing sets, press the polka dots onto the sides of the cake. For an even distribution, place two dots in a row, approximately 1 inch apart. Center another dot between these two, 1 inch to the right. Continue this pattern around the side of the cake. On top center a line of polka dots down the middle of the cake. Place another line of polka dots on each side, offset from but parallel to the first line. Repeat until the top is covered.

6. Adhere the cardboard round supporting the cake to your base. Press shavings of chocolate sprinkles around the bottom of the cake.

CHOCOLATE CHIP POUND CAKE

The secret of our unbelievably moist and delicious pound cake is cream cheese. For casual entertaining, this cake can be baked in a Bundt pan and simply dusted with confectioners' sugar or iced with Chocolate Glaze. Pound cake is an unexpected but surprisingly good choice for wedding and special-occasion cakes. Here's a Bakehouse trick: Both this and the Lemon Ginger Cream Cheese Pound Cake batter can be frozen in their prepared pans. Bring them to room temperature before baking.

Grease and flour a 2½-quart Bundt pan or kugelhopf mold or two 9 × 2-inch round pans. Preheat the oven to 350° F. Have all ingredients at room temperature.

In the bowl of an electric mixer, beat at high speed until light and fluffy:

8 ounces (2 sticks) unsalted butter

Add and beat well at high speed:

8 ounces cream cheese

Add and cream at high speed until light and fluffy:

1½ cups sugar

Add and mix well at medium speed:

2 tablespoons sour cream

1 teaspoon pure vanilla extract

Add one at a time, mixing well after each addition:

4 large eggs

On a piece of wax paper, sift together:

2¼ cups cake flour

2 teaspoons baking powder

¼ teaspoon salt

Add the dry ingredients to the butter and egg mixture and beat on low speed until smooth.

Stir in by hand:

1 cup semisweet chocolate chips

For the Bundt or kugelhopf pan, pour the batter into the pan and bake 45 to 55 minutes or until a cake tester inserted into the center comes out clean. Cool on a wire rack for 15 minutes before turning out of the pan. Cool completely.

For the 9-inch round pans, put a scant 3 cups in one pan and the remaining batter in the other. Bake the less full pan for 25 to 30 minutes and the fuller pan for 30 to 35 minutes, or until a cake tester comes out clean. Cool the cakes on wire racks for 15 minutes before turning them out of their pans.

Yield: 8 cups of batter

LEMON GINGER CREAM CHEESE POUND CAKE

The combination of lemon and ginger makes this cake a great choice for any summer party. Fill it with Lemon Mousse (page 61) or French custard (page 87) and raspberries and you will get rave reviews. For a picnic, try baking it in a Bundt pan. While it is baking, in a bowl whisk together ¼ cup lemon juice and 2 cups confectioners' sugar to make a tangy and sweet lemon glaze. Glaze the cake while it is still hot.

Grease and flour a 2½-quart Bundt pan or kugelhopf mold or two 9 × 2-inch round pans. Preheat the oven to 350°F. Have all ingredients at room temperature.

In the bowl of an electric mixer, beat at high speed until light and fluffy:

 8 ounces (2 sticks) unsalted butter

Add and beat well at high speed:

 8 ounces cream cheese

Add and cream until light and fluffy:

 1½ cups sugar

Add one at a time, mixing well after each addition:

 4 large eggs

Add and beat on low speed just to incorporate:

 2 tablespoons fresh lemon juice

 1½ tablespoons grated lemon zest

 1 teaspoon pure vanilla extract

On a piece of wax paper, sift together:

 2¼ cups cake flour

 2 teaspoons baking powder

 ¼ teaspoon salt

 1½ teaspoons ground ginger

Add the dry ingredients to the butter and egg mixture and mix on low speed until smooth.

Stir in by hand:

 1 cup (6 ounces) finely chopped crystallized ginger

For the Bundt or kugelhopf pan, pour the batter into the pan and bake 45 to 55 minutes, or until a cake tester inserted into the center comes out clean. Cool on a wire rack for 15 minutes before turning out of the pan. Pour the lemon glaze, if using (see note above), and cool completely.

For the 9-inch round pans, use a scant 3 cups to fill one pan and pour the remaining batter into the other. Bake the less full pan for 25 to 30 minutes and the fuller pan for 30 to 35 minutes, or until a cake tester comes out clean. Cool the cakes for 15 minutes before turning them out of their pans.

Yield: 8 cups of batter

WHIPPED CHOCOLATE GANACHE

We use Whipped Chocolate Ganache instead of chocolate mousse because it is simple to make, whips up easily, and tastes delicious. Unwhipped, it will stay fresh for 2 weeks in your refrigerator.

Add thin layers of melted chocolate to your cake layers before filling for a wonderful and unexpected crunch that contrasts nicely with the creamy whipped ganache.

Melt in a bowl over hot water:

   ½ pound semisweet chocolate

In a saucepan, bring to a boil:

   1 quart heavy cream

Whisk one third of the cream into the chocolate until smooth. Slowly whisk in the remaining cream. Refrigerate overnight or freeze for a few hours.

Whip until stiff.

Yield: 4¾ cups of filling when whipped

LEMON CURD

I was the pastry chef for Café Evergreen, whose owner, Dan Coon, loved lemon tarts, so I was always on the lookout for new ways to make lemon curd. I tried many recipes, and this was the keeper. The tangy curd is great by itself or in a lemon meringue pie. However, lemon curd on its own is too unstable to use as a cake filling, so we fold whipped cream into it, yielding a light, tart mousse. For a more intense lemon flavor, try spreading a thin layer of the curd on the cake layers before filling with the lemon mousse. Lemon curd must be prepared 4 hours in advance.

In a saucepan, bring to a boil:

> ½ cup strained fresh lemon juice
>
> ½ cup sugar
>
> 3 ounces (¾ stick) unsalted butter
>
> 1 tablespoon grated lemon zest

In the bowl of an electric mixer at medium speed, beat well:

> 4 large eggs

Slowly whisk the hot juice mixture into the eggs. Return the mixture to the saucepan and cook over medium-low heat, whisking constantly, until it coats the back of a spoon. Do not let the mixture boil or it will curdle.

Pour the curd through a strainer into a bowl. Place plastic wrap directly on the surface of the curd and refrigerate until cold. To chill the curd quickly, place the bowl over a bowl of ice and stir until cold.

Yield: 1½ cups

Variation
LEMON MOUSSE:

To yield 4½ cups of Lemon Mousse, whip 1½ cups heavy cream together with 2 tablespoons of confectioners' sugar until stiff. Gently fold in ¾ cup Lemon Curd. Use the remaining curd to make Lemon Buttercream (page 38) or to spread on cake layers.

Mini Birthday Cake

If the Cat in the Hat were a baker, this is what his specialty might look like. It is probably our most popular cake—we make more than 100 a week in two different sizes—and it has become our signature design. The first incarnation of the Mini Birthday Cake was true to its name—a 4-inch round cake—but soon we were making them in all sizes, and even stacking them up to five tiers high (see page 118). If you prefer not to work with as many colors as we show here, try some of these alternatives: a glazed background, tone on tone (such as light pink to dark pink), or all white.

What you will need:

Cake: one 10-inch round cake of your choice (we recommend Chocolate Butter Cake, page 65)

Filling: Cookies and Cream (page 65)

Icing: Kaye's Buttercream (page 37) or House Buttercream (page 36)

Decoration: 1 to 2 cups white wafer chocolate to make assorted chocolate candles

Colors: Teal, green, yellow, blue, violet, neon pink, and orange liquid gel colors and neon bright pink, green, blue, or violet candy colors (plus yellow)

Tips: #102 and #104 petal tip, #18 and #199 star tip, and #4 round tip

How to:

1. Bake the cake and let it cool completely. Prepare the filling and icing. Fill and crumb coat the cake as directed on pages 30–32. Chill the filled cake.

2. Melt 1 to 2 cups of white wafer chocolate. Set aside ¼ cup of melted chocolate. Using the Color Mixing Chart on page 26, tint the chocolate with your choice of candy color. Pour the chocolate into a pastry cone and cut a medium-size hole. On a sheet pan lined with parchment paper pipe out as many 5-inch candles as you will need. They should be at least ¼ inch wide and ⅛ inch thick. Set aside to harden.

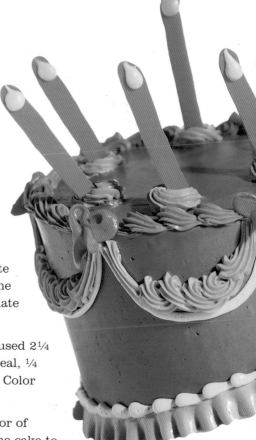

3. Tint the reserved chocolate yellow. Pour the chocolate into a pastry cone and cut a medium-size hole. When the candles are hard, flip them over and pipe yellow chocolate flames on their tips.

4. Prepare the colored buttercream of your choice; we used 2¼ cups purple, ¾ cup orange, ¾ cup lime green, ¼ cup teal, ¼ cup neon pink, ¼ cup blue, and ¼ cup yellow. (See the Color Mixing Chart on page 26.)

5. Ice the cake with purple buttercream or the base color of your choice. Adhere the cardboard round supporting the cake to your base.

6. Place the orange buttercream in a pastry bag with a coupler, and with a petal tip pipe or a Ruffled Ribbon Border (page 67) around the bottom edge.

7. Place the yellow or blue buttercream in a pastry bag with a coupler. Pipe a Bead Border (page 67) above the Ruffled Ribbon Border. With the same tip, pipe yellow linear swags. Place the lime-green buttercream in a pastry bag with a coupler, and with a star tip pipe lime-green Spiral Swags (page 68) using the swag lines as a guide. With the same tip, pipe an evenly spaced ring of rosettes around the outer edge of the cake top. There should be the same number of rosettes as there are candles.

8. Place the teal buttercream in a pastry bag with a coupler, and with a star tip pipe a shell border around the top edge.

9. Stick the chocolate candles into the rosettes so the flat sides face the front, pressing them halfway into the cake.

10. Place the neon pink in a pastry bag with a coupler, and with a petal tip pipe bows where the swags meet.

CHOCOLATE BUTTER CAKE

Classic, moist, and delicious, this versatile cake is sure to please any die-hard chocoholic or party of screaming kids. It is the most popular cake at the Bakehouse.

Grease and flour two 10 × 3-inch round pans. Preheat the oven to 350°F.

In a bowl, combine and whisk until there are no lumps:

> **1 cup hot coffee**
>
> **1 cup cocoa powder**

Add and whisk until smooth:

> **1 cup cold water**

On a piece of wax paper, sift together:

> **3 cups cake flour**
>
> **2 teaspoons baking soda**
>
> **½ teaspoon baking powder**
>
> **¾ teaspoon salt**

In the bowl of an electric mixer, beat at high speed until light and fluffy:

> **8 ounces (2 sticks) unsalted butter**
>
> **2½ cups sugar**

On medium speed, add slowly and cream well:

> **4 large eggs**
>
> **1½ teaspoons pure vanilla extract**

Add the dry ingredients alternately to the butter and egg mixture with the cocoa, mixing until smooth.

Pour 3 cups of the batter into one 10-inch pan and the remaining batter into the other 10-inch pan. Bake the less full pan for 20 to 25 minutes and the fuller pan for 30 to 35 minutes, or until a cake tester inserted into the center of the cake comes out clean. Cool the cakes on a wire rack for 15 to 20 minutes before turning them out of their pans.

Yield: 9 cups of batter

COOKIES AND CREAM

Yum, yum, yum. You might think this is for kids only, but adults love it just as much. We have even used cookies and cream as a wedding-cake filling. It is simply delicious.

In the bowl of an electric mixer at high speed, whip until stiff:

> **2½ cups heavy cream**
>
> **¼ cup confectioners' sugar**
>
> **½ teaspoon pure vanilla extract**

Gently fold in:

> **20 chocolate sandwich cookies, such as Oreos, crushed into medium pieces**

Yield: 6 cups

Piping

Depending on the piping application you choose you will need to adjust the consistency of your icing. Soft buttercream flows easily without air pockets and breaks, making it best for fine piping, lines, and inscriptions. Borders, rosettes, and swags need a medium-consistency buttercream that is fluid yet holds its form. Roses and other flowers need a firmer frosting for the petals to retain their shape. To make the buttercream firmer, chill it in the refrigerator for a few minutes, stirring often so the buttercream does not solidify. Conversely, to make the buttercream softer, lightly melt it over a double boiler, stirring constantly until the buttercream is soft and smooth.

The thickness and uniformity of your piping will be influenced by how much pressure you apply to the bag and the steadiness of that pressure. Twisting the top of the pastry bag creates a natural pressure. Squeezing the bag applies additional pressure and allows you to control the flow. Use one hand to guide the bag while squeezing with the other, twisting the top of the bag occasionally to maintain pressure. Your goal is to apply consistent pressure while moving the tip or bag at a steady pace or rhythm.

For most piping applications the pastry bag is held at a 45-degree angle to the cake. To begin, touch the pastry tip to the surface of the cake where you want to start piping, allowing the icing to adhere to the surface. Lift up the tip as you begin to apply pressure. Do not drag the tip along the surface of the cake; lightly touch the surface of the cake or hover above it as you pipe.

At the end of a line or embellishment stop applying pressure to the bag and quickly spiral the tip or pull the tip downward to the side. This is known as tailing off.

ROSETTES	DOTS
Star tip	**Round tip**

Hold the bag perpendicular to the surface of the cake. Using consistent pressure, pipe a tight circle. Without releasing the pressure, continue the spiral over the first circle, releasing the pressure as you tail it off.

Hold the bag perpendicular to the cake surface. Keeping the tip stationary, apply consistent pressure until the dot is the desired size. Release the pressure and tail off gently to the side or in a spiral to give a rounded finish.

BEAD BORDER OR SHELL BORDER

Round tip or star tip

A bead border is the same as a shell border, except that a round tip is used. Vary the pressure or tip size to make different-sized beads. Hold the bag at a 45-degree angle to the cake surface. Rest the tip where you are going to begin piping the bead. Without moving the bag, apply heavy, consistent pressure, allowing the tip to rise as the icing builds. Once the bead has formed, decrease the pressure while dragging the tip downward, forming a tail. Begin the next bead overlapping the tail of the first.

CRAZY CURLS

Round tip

This whimsical take on a traditional cornelli lace pattern is made with a fine tip and a continuous line. Hold the tip perpendicular to the cake surface. Touch the tip to the surface where you want to begin piping, then lift the tip up as you begin to apply pressure, moving the pastry bag randomly in a series of partially overlapping spirals, loops, and curls. To end the line, touch the tip to the surface of the cake again and discontinue the pressure.

RICKRACK BORDER

Petal tip

Hold the bag at a 45-degree angle to the cake surface for a flared rickrack or perpendicular to the cake surface for a flush rickrack. With the wide end of the tip up and lightly touching the cake, apply consistent pressure, moving the bag up and down in a tight zigzag motion.

PLAID

Flat and round tips

Hold the bag at a 45-degree angle to the cake surface. Pipe widely spaced equidistant parallel lines. Apply one or more additional sets of lines among the first, varying the color and tips (round and flat) to form a pattern. Perpendicular to these lines, pipe equidistant parallel lines. For plaid on the side of a cake, begin piping at the top edge. Lightly touching the cake, pipe equidistant, parallel, vertical lines flush with the cake surface. Stop applying pressure at the bottom and pull away. Pipe equidistant parallel horizontal lines, letting the icing flow naturally over the vertical row of lines. To disguise the takeoff and end points, finish the plaid by piping a line around the top border.

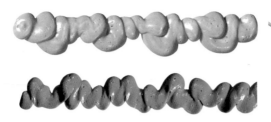

CRAZY BORDER OR CLOUD BORDER

Petal tip or round tip

Hold the bag at a 45-degree angle to the cake surface. With the wide end of the tip up and lightly touching the cake, apply inconsistent pressure while moving the bag up and down randomly.

RUFFLED RIBBON BORDER

Petal tip

Hold the bag at a 45-degree angle to the cake surface. With the wide end of the tip up and lightly touching the cake, apply consistent pressure, moving the tip up and down while simultaneously raising and lowering the narrow end of the tip as you move around the cake, giving the illusion of subtle, overlapping ruffles.

THREAD SWAGS AND LINES

Round tip

Trace the swags onto the cake surface with a toothpick before piping. For precise swags, divide the cake's circumference by six or eight, then mark off the points between the swags around the cake. Holding the bag perpendicular to the side of the cake, lightly touch the side of the cake, and with consistent light pressure, pipe a string from the top edge, down through the arch, then up to the top again. Allow the icing to drape naturally in an arc, lightly touching the surface of the cake.

SPIRAL SWAGS

Star tip

Trace the swags with a toothpick before piping. For precise swags divide the cake's circumference by six or eight, then mark off the points between the swags around the cake. Hold the bag at a 45-degree angle to the side of the cake. Lightly touching the cake, begin piping in a tight spiral motion from the top, arching down and then up to the top edge again. Apply more pressure at the belly of the arc to give a fuller swag, tailing off at the ends.

LATTICE

Flat tip

Hold the bag at a 45-degree angle to the cake surface. Pipe equidistant parallel lines. At a 45°–60° angle to these lines, pipe equidistant parallel lines. For lattice on the side of a cake, begin piping at the top edge. Lightly touching the cake at a 30-degree angle, pipe equidistant parallel lines flush with the cake surface. At the bottom stop applying pressure and pull away. In the opposite direction pipe equidistant parallel lines, letting the icing flow naturally over the first row of lattice. To disguise the takeoff and end points, finish the lattice by piping a line around the top border.

BASKET WEAVE

Basket-weave tip

Hold the bag at a 45-degree angle to the cake surface. With the grooved edge pointing up, pipe a vertical line where you want to begin the basket weave. Pipe equidistant horizontal lines, separated by the width of the tip, overlapping the vertical line by ½ inch on each side. Approximately ¼ inch to the right of the first vertical line, and slightly overlapping the horizontal lines, pipe another vertical line. Pipe another set of horizontal lines, starting in the empty spaces formed between the first set of horizontal lines, overlapping the second vertical line by ½ inch.

BOWS

Petal tip

Hold the bag at a 45-degree angle to the cake surface. With the wide end of the tip pointed down, squeeze, moving the tip up and around to the right, ending at the starting point. Then, starting at the same point, squeeze, moving the tip up and around to the left, again ending at the starting point. (You can also pipe this portion of the bow in one fluid figure-eight motion). At the starting point, squeeze two ribbons down to finish off the bow.

FLAT RIBBON

Petal tip

Hold the bag at a 45-degree angle to the cake surface. With the wide end of the tip down, apply consistent pressure while piping a ribbon flush to the cake surface. Keep the narrow end lightly brushing the surface of the cake to ensure that it adheres.

For a slightly flared, flat ribbon, the reverse can be done, piping with the wide end up and always touching the cake, and the narrow end at a 15-degree angle to the cake.

Crazy Swirls

Dizzying and delightful, crazy swirls are a breeze to make. This freewheeling decorative effect is also very versatile; use a smaller tip to pipe the swirls for a more refined cake, or switch to a larger round tip and get as chunky and fun as you want. Marbleized buttercream adds a layer of interest to this rather basic embellishment, but a solid color or tone-on-tone works just as well. You can even reverse the design and pipe colored swirls on a white background.

What you will need:

Cake: one 9-inch round cake of your choice (we recommend the Walnut Caramel Cake or the Hazelnut Cake, both on the next page)

Filling: 4 cups of your choice of filling (we recommend Coffee Mousse or Chocolate Hazelnut Mousse, both on page 100)

Icing: Kaye's Buttercream (page 37) or House Buttercream (page 36)

Colors: Orange, red, and yellow liquid-gel colors (page 26)

Tips: #4, #5, #6, or #7 round tip

How to:

1. Bake the cake and let it cool completely. Prepare the filling and icing. Fill and crumb coat the cake as directed on pages 30–32. Chill the filled cake.

2. Set aside 2 cups of uncolored buttercream. Using the Color Mixing Chart on page 26, prepare the tinted buttercream: ½ cup each of pale yellow, yellow, yellow-orange, orange, peach, and orange-red. With the metal spatula press thick dollops of each color randomly around the cake, covering the crumb coat. This can be as messy as you want, but try to keep each color block pure; don't let it bleed into its neighbor. Chill the cake again, until the buttercream is firm to the touch.

3. With a hot metal spatula (dip in hot water, and dry off), scrape off the excess buttercream to make the cake smooth, using the cardboard round as a guide. The color blocks should remain as they were first applied without running into one another and muting. If there are any empty spots, fill them in with any remaining tinted buttercream and smooth with a spatula.

4. Adhere the cardboard round supporting the cake to your base.

5. Place the reserved, uncolored buttercream in a pastry bag with a coupler, and with a round tip pipe swirls covering the entire cake surface. Pipe a crazy curl border (page 67) around the bottom edge of the cake (see pages 66–69 for more piping borders).

WALNUT CARAMEL CAKE

Fill this wonderful, buttery, walnut-studded cake with anything from homemade applesauce (which is how we fill it at Thanksgiving time) to chocolate mousse or coffee mousse.

Grease two 9 × 3-inch round pans. Preheat the oven to 350° F. Have all ingredients at room temperature.

In the bowl of an electric mixer, beat at high speed until light and fluffy:

   6 ounces (1½ sticks) unsalted butter

   1½ cups light brown sugar, packed

Add one at a time and beat well:

   3 large eggs

On a piece of wax paper, sift together:

   3 cups cake flour

   1 tablespoon baking powder

   ¾ teaspoon salt

At low speed add the dry ingredients to the butter and egg mixture alternately with:

   1 cup milk

Stir in by hand:

   1½ cups chopped walnuts

Pour 3 cups of the batter into one prepared pan and the remaining batter into the other. Bake the less full pan for 20 to 25 minutes and the fuller pan for 30 to 35 minutes, or until a cake tester inserted into the center of the cake comes out clean. Cool the cakes on a wire rack for 15 to 20 minutes before turning them out of the pans.

Yield: 7½ cups of batter

HAZELNUT CAKE

I recently came across this recipe from twenty-five years ago that I had found written in a composition book of my favorite recipes. It was called Filbert Cake and had only one problem: It called for shortening. Once I substituted butter, everyone flipped over it. It is worth the trip to the gourmet store for the Nutella to make the mousse filling for this cake.

Grease two 8×3-inch round pans. Preheat the oven to 350° F. Have all ingredients at room temperature.

In the bowl of an electric mixer, beat at high speed until light and fluffy:

> 4 ounces (1 stick) unsalted butter
>
> 1½ cups brown sugar, packed

Add and beat until combined:

> 2 large eggs

On a piece of wax paper, sift together:

> 1¾ cups all-purpose flour
>
> ½ teaspoon salt
>
> ½ teaspoon baking powder
>
> 1 teaspoon baking soda

Add the dry ingredients to the butter and egg mixture alternately with:

> 1¼ cups sour cream

Beat until smooth, then stir in by hand:

> ⅔ cup finely chopped toasted hazelnuts

Pour 3 cups of the batter into one prepared pan and the remaining batter into the other. Bake the less full pan for 20 to 25 minutes and the fuller pan for 30 to 35 minutes, or until a cake tester inserted into the center of the cake comes out clean. Cool on a wire rack for 15 to 20 minutes before turning the cakes out of the pans.

Note: To toast hazelnuts, place the nuts on an ungreased sheet pan. Bake at 350°F. for 12 to 18 minutes, or until the skins are cracked and the nuts are golden. Let cool, then rub the nuts together in a towel to remove the skins.

Yield: 5 cups of batter

Bugged Out

Kids are fascinated by bugs and they don't get many chances to eat them, so these cupcakes are always a hit. Our chubby bumblebee and his friends are made using the Multicolor Chocolate Method (page 78); sprinkles and nonpareils add to the festive buzz. As an alternative to the chocolate decorations, you can simply roll a glazed cupcake in red nonpareil sprinkles, then pipe on a head and spots with melted chocolate to create a cute ladybug. Pipe on eyes with buttercream or melted white chocolate.

What you will need:

Cake: Vanilla Cupcakes (page 77) or Chocolate Cupcakes (page 76)

Icing: House Buttercream (page 36) and/or Chocolate Glaze (page 35)

Decoration: 3 cups of white wafer chocolate and 3 cups of dark wafer chocolate to make 12 to 24 chocolate bugs

Colors: green, blue, and yellow liquid gel colors

Colored sprinkles, nonpareils, and chocolate sprinkles

How to:

1. Using the templates provided, make 12 to 24 bugs with the wafer chocolate as illustrated in the Multicolor Chocolate Method on page 78.

2. Bake the cupcakes and let them cool completely. I recommend freezing the cupcakes; they are easier to handle in this state and the glaze sets quickly.

3. Prepare the Chocolate Glaze and/or the House Buttercream.

4. If using Chocolate Glaze, dip the top of the frozen cupcake in the glaze up to its paper liner. Shake lightly, and place the coated cupcake on parchment paper. Before the glaze has set completely, roll the edge or the entire cupcake in sprinkles. Experiment with different colored sprinkles.

5. If using buttercream, mix a variety of colors. Use a metal spatula to ice the cupcakes. Roll the edges in sprinkles.

6. Pipe a dot of buttercream on the underside of each chocolate bug to give it a high perch. Place the bugs on the cupcakes, pressing lightly to adhere.

CHOCOLATE CUPCAKES

Contrary to popular belief, not just any cake recipe will work for cupcakes. This batter is easy to make and rises beautifully, and children and adults alike love the results. Around Halloween at the Bakehouse, we top them with spooky designs, like spiders and skeletons.

Grease the tops of two 12-cup cupcake pans and line the pans with cupcake liners. Preheat the oven to 350°F. Have all ingredients at room temperature.

In a saucepan, melt together over low heat, whisking often:

   ½ cup milk

   1 cup brown sugar, packed

   3 ounces unsweetened chocolate

When the chocolate is melted, whisk in:

   1 large egg yolk

Remove from the heat and set aside.

In the bowl of an electric mixer at medium-high speed, cream:

   4 ounces (1 stick) unsalted butter

Add and cream until light and fluffy:

   1 cup granulated sugar

Add slowly, beating well and scraping down after each addition:

   2 large eggs

   1 large egg white

On a piece of wax paper, sift together:

   2 cups cake flour

   1 teaspoon baking soda

   ½ teaspoon salt

On low speed add the dry ingredients alternately to the butter and egg mixture with:

   ¾ cup milk

   1 teaspoon pure vanilla extract

Stir the chocolate mixture into the batter by hand, mixing only until combined.

Pour the batter into the cupcake liners, filling each seven-eighths full. Bake 18 to 20 minutes, or until the tops springs back when lightly pressed.

Yield: 18 to 20 cupcakes

VANILLA CUPCAKES

Cupcakes are not just for kids' parties anymore. At the Bakehouse we make them for Mother's Day, Super Bowl Sunday, Valentine's Day, and even weddings. This recipe can be successfully doubled or quadrupled, and the cupcakes freeze beautifully.

Grease the top of a 12-cup cupcake pan and line it with cupcake liners. Preheat the oven to 350° F. Have all ingredients at room temperature.

Sift into a mixing bowl:

   1¾ cups plus 2 tablespoons cake flour

   ¾ teaspoon salt

Add and mix to combine:

   1 cup sugar

Add:

   ½ cup plus 2½ teaspoons warmed milk (110° F.)

   2 large eggs

   4 ounces (1 stick) very soft unsalted butter

   ½ teaspoon pure vanilla extract

Beat at low speed with the whisk attachment for 1 minute. Scrape down the bowl. Raise the speed to medium-low and beat for 1½ minutes.

Add:

   1½ teaspoons baking powder

Mix at low speed for 30 seconds.

Fill each liner three-quarters full. Bake 18 to 20 minutes, or until golden. The tops should spring back when lightly pressed.

Yield: 12 cupcakes

Multicolor Chocolate Method

These colorful bugs are a fun illustration of how multiple colors can be combined with a bold chocolate outline for a cartoon-like effect. I begin by drawing a defined outline with chocolate, and I fill in this outline with color, being careful to stay within the lines. Don't worry if you go outside the lines a little; the initial outline will maintain the definition of the design. In most cases pure chocolate stands in for the color black, whether it is a line or it fills in a form. For more sophisticated designs, try outlining in color instead of black, or do not use any outline at all; let the colors run right up to one another. To prevent the decoration from breaking along the seams, it is important that the colors overlap.

What you will need:

Sheet pan

Parchment paper

1/2 cup dark wafer chocolate and 1 cup white
wafer chocolate (makes approximately 10 bumblebees)

Yellow and blue candy colors (Optional: to make
other bugs, use red, purple, green, and orange candy colors)

Pastry cones

Small plastic bowls

Rubber spatulas

How to:

1. Photocopy or trace the bumblebee template. Tape the template onto a sheet pan or a flat surface. Cover the template with parchment paper.

2. Melt the dark and white chocolate. Split the melted white chocolate between two bowls. Tint one bowl of white chocolate yellow and the other blue. Pour the colored and dark chocolates into 3 separate pastry cones.

3. Cut a small hole in the dark chocolate pastry cone to release a fine line. Use the dark chocolate to trace the outline of the bee and fill in all areas that are black, including the two dots for the eyes.

4. Cut a medium-size hole in the yellow pastry cone to release a somewhat thicker line of chocolate. Fill in the body of the bee, starting close to the outline but not touching it. Let the chocolate flow up to the outline by itself, pushing it with the tip if need be. Make sure the yellow overlaps the black body stripes; this will prevent the design from breaking along the seams. The chocolate should be approximately ⅛ inch thick, but it can be thicker. If the design is much thinner, however, it will be too fragile to handle.

5. Cut a medium-size hole in the blue pastry cone. Fill in the blue wings in the same manner, again making sure to overlap part of the body. You can gently tap on the pan to help the chocolate settle into the outlines. Try not to cover the outlines with the colored chocolate but if you do, don't worry, the outline will maintain the definition of the form. Set aside to harden.

6. When the chocolate has set, gently flip the design and carefully peel off the parchment paper to reveal your bumblebee.

Summer Nights

There is something magical about a field of fireflies at night. To a child, chasing their glow with cupped hands is simultaneously frightening and wonderful. This cake pays homage to those nights of wide-eyed innocence. The variegated buttercream icing brings the sky and the earth together in an ethereal blend of colors; it's an easy effect to achieve that creates a pleasantly surreal background against which to place decorations.

What you will need:

Cake: one 9-inch round cake of your choice (we recommend the Banana Cake, page 86, or the Pinwheel Cake, page 84)

Filling: French Custard (page 87) for Banana Cake or Pinwheel Filling (page 85) for Pinwheel Cake

Icing: Kaye's Buttercream (page 37) or House Buttercream (page 36)

Decoration: ½ cup dark wafer chocolate and 1 to 2 cups white wafer chocolate to make 12 large and 12 small chocolate fireflies and 1 large and 3 small chocolate moons

Colors: royal blue, violet, green, and yellow liquid gel colors; sky blue, yellow, green, and orange candy colors

Tips: #104 petal tip (#103 or #102 can be substituted) and #7 round tip (#6, #5, or #4 can be substituted)

How to:

1. Bake the cake and let it cool completely. Prepare the filling and icing. Fill and crumb coat the layers as directed on pages 30–32. Chill the filled cake.

2. Melt the white and dark chocolates. Using the photographs on this page and opposite as templates, pipe out approximately 12 large and 12 small fireflies as illustrated in the Multicolor Method (page 78). Set aside to harden.

3. Fill a fine-tipped pastry cone with melted dark chocolate. Make 1 large and 3 small moons by filling in a 4 × 4-inch area with delicate overlapping spirals, circles, and dots. Cut a large hole in a pastry cone filled with melted white chocolate and pipe out a 1½-inch dot over the chocolate drawing. Pipe out 2 or 3 more moons approximately ¾ inch in diameter. Set aside to harden.

4. Set aside ¼ cup of the white buttercream, then divide the remaining buttercream between 2 bowls. Using the Color Mixing Chart on page 26, tint one bowl of buttercream midnight blue and the other lime green.

5. Place the cake on a turntable. Spread a 1-inch band of lime-green buttercream around the base of the cake. Cover the remainder of the cake with midnight blue. Dip a flat metal spatula or scraper into hot water, wipe it dry, then, while spinning the turntable, run the heated spatula or scraper around the side of the cake using the cardboard round as your guide. The colors will blend into each other.

6. Adhere the cardboard round supporting the cake to your base.

7. Place the remaining lime-green buttercream in a pastry bag with a coupler, and with a petal tip pipe a Crazy Border (page 67) around the bottom edge.

8. Change to a round tip and pipe twenty-four ¼-inch dots randomly around the top and sides of the cake. Heat an offset spatula in hot water, dry it off, and press down on each dot to melt it into the night sky. Lift the spatula away by gliding it to the side; don't pull straight up. Reheat the spatula for each dot.

9. While the buttercream is still soft, stick the lightning bugs' tails on the glowing dots. Gently press their tails down, so their bodies appear to rise in flight.

10. Fill a small pastry cone with the reserved white buttercream. Choose a front for the cake, then pipe a 2½-inch spiral in the upper left quadrant. With a heated offset metal spatula gently flatten the spiral, allowing it to blend with the background. Lift the spatula away by gliding it to the side. Put a dollop of midnight-blue buttercream on the underside of the large moon and place it right side up in the upper left-hand portion of the cake. Gently press the front edge of the moon down, tilting the back upward. Using dabs of buttercream, apply the small moons to the sides of the cake, spacing them evenly.

PINWHEEL CAKE

My mother claimed to have found the recipe on the back of a chocolate box; whatever its origins, it was a beloved birthday tradition for her entire family. In contrast to the Chocolate Butter Cake (page 65), this cake is light in color. We like it filled with a chocolate buttercream (see Pinwheel Filling, page 85), and though my mother served it un-iced, allowing the baked-in swirl of chocolate to reflect the cake's simplicity, you can certainly ice it and add any number of the other designs.

Grease two 8 × 3-inch round pans. Preheat the oven to 350°F. Have all ingredients at room temperature.

Sift into the bowl of an electric mixer:

> 2 cups cake flour
>
> 1½ cups sugar
>
> 2 teaspoons baking powder
>
> ¼ teaspoon baking soda
>
> 1 teaspoon salt

Add to the mixing bowl and beat on low speed with the paddle attachment for 2 minutes:

> 4 ounces (1 stick) softened unsalted butter
>
> 1 cup evaporated milk
>
> 1 teaspoon pure vanilla extract

Add and continue to mix on low speed for 1½ minutes:

> 2 large eggs
>
> ¼ cup evaporated milk
>
> 2 ounces unsweetened chocolate, melted and cooled

In a separate bowl have ready:

> 1 ounce unsweetened chocolate, melted and cooled

Divide the batter equally between the prepared pans. Drizzle the additional ounce of melted unsweetened chocolate over the batter in each pan. Using a paring knife or a cake tester, make a circular pattern in the batter. This will create the pinwheel effect. Bake the cakes for 20 to 25 minutes, or until a cake tester inserted into the center of the cake comes out clean. Cool the cakes on a wire rack for 15 to 20 minutes before turning them out of their pans. Cool completely, before filling and icing.

Cut each cake layer in half horizontally. Place the bottom layer on a cardboard round or cake plate. If you are filling the cake, spread one third of the Pinwheel Filling (page 85) evenly on the bottom layer. Top with a second layer and repeat with the remaining filling and layers, with a pinwheel design on top.

Yield: 6 cups of batter

PINWHEEL FILLING

Over the years I've replaced the shortening in this recipe with real butter so that it melts in your mouth.

In the bowl of an electric mixer, use the whisk attachment to beat together until light and fluffy:

    1 ounce unsweetened chocolate, melted and cooled

    8 ounces (2 sticks) softened unsalted butter

    ¾ cup confectioners' sugar

    2 tablespoons evaporated milk

    1 teaspoon pure vanilla extract

    a pinch of salt

Yield: 2 cups

BANANA CAKE

This moist, buttery, and banana-y cake is rich without being heavy. Fill this cake with French Custard (facing page) and pour Chocolate Glaze (page 39) over it and you will get rave reviews. I recently took it, along with five other cakes, to a party and it was the hands-down favorite.

Grease two 9 × 3-inch round pans. Preheat the oven to 350° F. Have all ingredients at room temperature.

In the bowl of an electric mixer, beat at high speed until light and fluffy:

8 ounces (2 sticks) softened unsalted butter

1½ cups brown sugar, firmly packed

½ cup granulated sugar

Add and beat well:

3 large eggs

Add:

2 cups mashed banana (about 3 large bananas)

The batter might look curdled; don't worry.

On a piece of wax paper, sift together:

3 cups cake flour

1½ teaspoons baking powder

¾ teaspoon salt

Mix the dry ingredients into the butter and egg mixture at low speed just until combined.

Pour 3 cups of the batter into one prepared pan and the remaining batter into the second pan. Bake the less full pan for 20 to 25 minutes and the fuller pan for 30 to 35 minutes, or until a cake tester inserted into the center of the cake comes out clean. Cool the cakes on a wire rack for 15 to 20 minutes before turning them out of their pans.

Yield: 8 cups of batter

FRENCH CUSTARD

French custard is pastry cream and whipped cream folded together, a filling that is not only more stable than pastry cream but also lighter.

One of my first recipes for pastry cream was from John Clancy, from whom I took classes years ago. I tweaked his recipe, adding more egg yolks to make the consistency firmer. On its own the pastry cream can be used as a filling for éclairs, cream puffs, fresh fruit tarts, or Boston cream pie. You should prepare the pastry cream in advance, but do not fold in the whipped cream until you are ready to put your cake together. This will make 1½ cups of pastry cream.

In a saucepan, bring to a boil:

1 cup milk

¼ vanilla bean (see Note)

In a bowl of an electric mixer, on medium speed, beat until light and fluffy:

3 large egg yolks

⅓ cup sugar

pinch of salt

Add and mix to combine:

2 tablespoons cornstarch

Remove the vanilla bean from the milk, then slowly beat the hot milk into the yolk mixture. Return the mixture to the saucepan. Return to a boil over medium-low heat, stirring constantly. Boil for 1 minute on low heat, stirring constantly.

Pour the pastry cream into a stainless-steel bowl and place over a bowl of ice water. Stir frequently until chilled. The cream will thicken as it cools. Alternately, cover the cream with plastic and refrigerate until cold.

In the bowl of an electric mixer, whip until stiff:

1½ cups heavy cream

2 tablespoons confectioners' sugar

Gently fold the chilled cream into the whipped cream.

Note: If you do not have a vanilla bean, substitute ¾ teaspoon pure vanilla extract. Add the vanilla when the pastry cream is removed from the heat.

Yield: 4½ cups

Sunflower

I've used many techniques to make sunflowers, including piping them in buttercream, but the one that tops this cake is the king of them all. This majestic sunflower's warm and earthy realism, set against the bright green field, *is* summer.

What you will need:

Cake: one 10-inch round cake of your choice (we recommend the Golden Butter Cake, page 91, or the Orange Butter Cake, page 90)

Filling: Orange Mousse (page 92)

Icing: Kaye's Buttercream (page 37) or House Buttercream (page 36)

Decoration: 1 chocolate sunflower with leaves and stem

Optional: 10 each chocolate daisies and daisies in perspective with stems and leaves

Colors: green and yellow liquid gel colors

Tips: #104 petal tip (#103 or #102 can be substituted) and #66 leaf tip

How to:

1. Bake the cake and let it cool completely. Prepare the filling and icing. Fill and crumb coat the layers as directed on pages 30–32. Chill the filled cake.

2. Using the template provided (see page 94) make a sunflower, plus stem and leaves as illustrated in the Advanced Chocolate Method. If you like, make 10 daisies and 10 daisies in perspective with stems and leaves, using the templates. Set aside to harden.

3. Using the Color Mixing Chart on page 26, tint the remaining buttercream lime green. Ice the cake. Adhere the cardboard circle supporting the cake to your base.

4. Place the remaining lime green buttercream in a pastry bag with a coupler, and with a petal tip pipe a Crazy Border (page 67) around the bottom edge.

5. Place the sunflower's stem on the cake top. Pipe a dab of buttercream onto the underside of the sunflower. Invert it and set it carefully overlapping the tip of the stem. Attach the leaves in the same fashion.

6. If desired, arrange the daisy stems around the sides of the cake. Add the flower heads, overlapping the stem tips, again adhering with buttercream dots. Fill in with leaves.

ORANGE BUTTER CAKE

One day, while experimenting with the Golden Butter Cake recipe (facing page), I was inspired to add some orange zest and orange juice. The resulting cake smelled delicious coming out of the oven, and filled with the orange mousse, it was unusually delicate and refreshing.

Grease two 10 × 3-inch round pans. Preheat the oven to 350°F. Have all ingredients at room temperature.

In the bowl of an electric mixer, beat at high speed until light and fluffy:

> 8 ounces (2 sticks) unsalted butter
>
> 2 cups sugar

Add and beat well:

> 6 large egg yolks
>
> 1½ teaspoons pure vanilla extract

On a piece of wax paper, sift together:

> 3½ cups cake flour
>
> 1 tablespoon plus ½ teaspoon baking powder
>
> ¾ teaspoon salt

Add the dry ingredients alternately to the butter and egg mixture with:

> ¾ cup milk
>
> ¾ cup strained fresh orange juice
>
> 1 tablespoon grated orange zest

Pour 3½ cups of the batter into one prepared pan and the remaining batter into the other. Bake the less full pan for 20 to 25 minutes and the fuller pan for 30 to 35 minutes, or until a cake tester inserted into the center of the cake comes out clean. Cool the cakes on a wire rack for 15 to 20 minutes before turning them out of their pans.

Yield: 9 cups of batter

GOLDEN BUTTER CAKE

This richly flavored butter and egg-yolk cake, an American classic, is perfect for any occasion. We use it for everything from Boston cream pie to wedding cakes and I can't think of any filling that would not be delicious with this very versatile cake.

Grease two 10 × 3-inch round pans. Preheat the oven to 350°F. Have all ingredients at room temperature.

In the bowl of an electric mixer, beat at high speed until light and fluffy:

    8 ounces (2 sticks) unsalted butter

    2 cups sugar

Add and beat on medium speed until fluffy:

    6 large egg yolks

    1½ teaspoons pure vanilla extract

On a piece of wax paper, sift together:

    3½ cups cake flour

    1 tablespoon plus ½ teaspoon baking powder

    ¾ teaspoon salt

At low speed, add the dry ingredients to the butter and egg mixture alternately with:

    1½ cups milk

Pour 3½ cups of the batter into one prepared pan and the remaining batter into the other. Bake the less full pan for 20 to 25 minutes and the fuller pan for 30 to 35 minutes, or until a cake tester inserted into the center of the cake comes out clean. Cool the cakes on a wire rack for 15 to 20 minutes before turning them out of their pans.

Yield: 9 cups of batter

ORANGE MOUSSE

This pastel cream, a relative of our Lemon Mousse (page 61), has a soft and subtle flavor. When you are filling a cake with orange mousse, spread thin layers of the plain curd on the cake layers to heighten the flavor and add moisture to the cake. You will need to prepare the orange curd in advance.

In a saucepan, combine and bring to a boil over medium heat:

1 cup milk

Grated zest of 1 orange

In the bowl of an electric mixer, beat at high speed until light and ribbons form when beaters are lifted:

3 large egg yolks

⅓ cup granulated sugar

4 tablespoons flour

Slowly whisk the hot milk into the eggs, then add:

½ cup strained fresh orange juice

Return to the saucepan and place over medium-low heat. Cook, stirring constantly, until the mixture boils, then boil for 1 minute, whisking constantly. Pour the curd into a container and place plastic wrap directly on the surface to prevent a skin from forming. Refrigerate. To chill quickly, whisk the orange curd over a bowl of ice water.

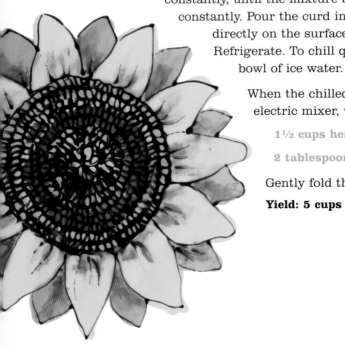

When the chilled curd is ready to use, in the bowl of an electric mixer, whip until stiff:

1½ cups heavy cream

2 tablespoons confectioners' sugar

Gently fold the chilled curd into the whipped cream.

Yield: 5 cups

Advanced Chocolate Method

A bit more intricate and sophisticated than the Multicolor Chocolate Method on page 78, this process enables you to create delicate and painterly designs by combining fine lines with highlights, shadows, and blending. You will be amazed at what realistic effects you can achieve using nothing more than melted chocolate! When I first started experimenting with the versatility of chocolate as a painting medium, I would clumsily blend it with a small offset spatula. Out of curiosity, I tried a paintbrush to see if it would work, and to my surprise it did. A portable stove that keeps the chocolate warm and melts the chocolate in the bristles of the brush became my palette, and candy colors my paints. If you do not have a portable stove or hot plate, try a double boiler with a shallow baking pan as its top. Clean the brush between colors by wiping it with a paper towel, or running it under hot water, melting away any chocolate in the bristles, and drying it thoroughly; you can also use several brushes.

What you will need:

Sheet pan

Parchment paper

½ cup dark wafer chocolate
and 2 cups white wafer chocolate

6 plastic bowls

Red, orange, yellow, and
green candy colors

Soft-bristled paintbrush
(I recommend a #1 or #2)

Pastry cones

Rubber spatulas

How to:

1. Photocopy the template to the desired size. Tape the template on a sheet pan or flat surface. Cover the template with parchment paper.

2. Melt ½ cup of dark chocolate and 2 cups of white chocolate.

3. Divide the white chocolate among 5 bowls (bowls 1 and 2 should have slightly more chocolate than bowls 3, 4, and 5). Tint the two fuller bowls yellow and orange and, using the Color Mixing Chart on page 26, tint the remaining three red-orange, autumn green, and burnt sienna. Pour the dark chocolate and the colored chocolates into 6 separate pastry cones.

4. Cut a very small hole in the dark chocolate pastry cone. With a fine line, trace the outline of the sunflower, including all of the seeds.

5. Still using the pastry cone of chocolate, pipe an additional line of chocolate around the edge of the seeds. Before it sets, use the paintbrush to gently feather the chocolate in the direction of the petal, working from the base to the tip. Pipe a dot of chocolate in the center of the sunflower and spread it with the paintbrush in a circular motion, being careful not to wipe off the seed lines. You should be able to still see the parchment through these semi-transparent "shadows."

6. With the red-orange, pipe thin lines around the edge of the outer petals where they touch the center petals. Use the brush to blend it toward the tip of each petal.

7. With the orange, pipe thin lines around the outer edge of the seeds. Use the brush to blend it toward the tip of the petals. Pipe an orange circle inside the seeds, halfway from the center, then gently blend the line into the seeds.

8. Fill in the center petals with yellow. Put a drop of yellow in the center of the sunflower and blend with the brush.

9. Fill in the outer petals with orange.

10. Pipe a ring of autumn green around the center of the sunflower. Blend gently with the paintbrush.

11. Fill in with burnt sienna, overlapping the colors for stability. Set aside to harden.

12. When hardened, carefully flip the design and gently peel off the parchment paper.

Winter Wonderland

Snowy-white chocolate decorations can evoke the pleasures of winter—sledding, making snow angels, and, of course, snowmen—all year long. This cake is a good illustration of how you can use false perspective to give cakes an appearance of depth and dimensionality. When the chocolate decorations are tilted forward they appear three-dimensional in a way that is reminiscent of a stage set or a shadowbox. To create a scene like this you must work in layers. Start at the back of the cake, playing with each design's angle as you work toward the foreground.

What you will need:

Cake: one 9-inch round cake (we recommend White Butter Cake, page 98

Filling: Raspberry Mousse (page 100)

Icing: House Buttercream (page 36) or Kaye's Buttercream (page 37)

Decoration: 1–2 cups of white wafer chocolate and ¼ cup of dark wafer chocolate to make:

    1 chocolate snowman

    6–8 chocolate pine trees

    30 chocolate polka dots

Colors: sky-blue liquid gel color

Tips: #104, #103, or #102 petal tip and #7 round tip

White chocolate shavings or finely grated coconut

Edible glitter

Green luster dust

How to:

1. Bake the cake and let it cool completely. Prepare the filling and icing. Fill and crumb coat the cake as directed on pages 30–32. Chill the filled cake.

2. Using the templates provided (see page 102) make a snowman, and 6 to 8 pine trees as illustrated in the Relief Chocolate Method. The trees are made with varying shades of green chocolate piped in relief on top of a chocolate tree. Make the polka dots. When the chocolate has set, dust the trees with green luster dust.

3. Set aside 1½ cups of the white buttercream. Tint the remaining buttercream ice blue. Ice the cake with the ice-blue buttercream. Adhere the cardboard round supporting the cake to your base.

4. Spread a thin layer of white buttercream on the front or lower half of the top.

5. Plant a few trees on the horizon, pressing at their base to tilt the tips upward.

6. Pipe buttercream onto the back of the snowman and place him in front of the trees, again pressing at the base to tilt him forward.

7. Press the polka dots onto the sides of the cake.

8. Place the remaining white buttercream into a pastry bag with a coupler, and with a petal tip pipe a Crazy Border, page 67, around the bottom edge of the cake.

9. Change to a round tip and pipe white icicles around the top edge as if they were hanging down the sides.

10. For a fresh dusting of snow, grate white chocolate over the scene. Sprinkle edible glitter on the cake to make the snow glisten.

WHITE BUTTER CAKE

When I began to take on freelance baking projects, Daniel Leder, who owns Bread Alone, gave me a great book called *The Modern Pastry Chef's Guide to Professional Baking*. My White Butter Cake is an adaptation of a recipe from that book. Fresh from the oven, this beautiful, dense white cake has a lovely, bouncy texture. It is a joy to work with and is wonderful to eat, especially filled with both lemon and raspberry mousses.

Grease two 10 × 3-inch round pans. Preheat the oven to 350°F. Have all ingredients at room temperature.

In the bowl of an electric mixer, beat at high speed until light and fluffy:

> 6 ounces (1½ sticks) unsalted butter
>
> 2 cups sugar
>
> 1½ teaspoons salt

On a piece of wax paper, sift together:

> 3⅓ cups cake flour
>
> 1½ teaspoons baking powder
>
> ¾ teaspoon cream of tartar

Add the dry ingredients to the butter mixture alternately with:

> 1¼ cups milk
>
> ¾ teaspoon pure vanilla extract

In a separate bowl beat until foamy:

> ¾ cup egg whites (6 to 8 large egg whites)

Continue beating at high speed while gradually adding:

> ½ cup sugar

When stiff peaks form, fold the whites into the cake batter with a rubber spatula. Blend just until the whites are evenly distributed.

Pour 3½ cups of the batter into one prepared pan and the remaining batter into the other. Bake the less full pan for 20 to 25 minutes and the fuller pan for 30 to 35 minutes, or until a cake tester inserted into the center of the cake comes out clean. Cool the cakes on a wire rack for 15 to 20 minutes before turning them out of their pans.

Yield: 9 cups of batter

SPICE CAKE

Unlike many children, Liv wasn't partial to chocolate cake as a child, so I always made this spice cake for her birthday. As it bakes it fills the air with the most wonderful aroma of butter and spices. You will find it as difficult as I do to refrain from eating it before it has time to cool completely.

Grease two 9 × 3-inch round pans. Preheat the oven to 350°F. Have all ingredients at room temperature.

In the bowl of an electric mixer, beat at high speed until light and fluffy:

> 9 ounces (2 sticks plus 2 tablespoons) unsalted butter
>
> 1½ cups sugar

Add at medium speed and beat until well creamed:

> 4 large egg yolks

On a piece of wax paper, sift together:

> 3 cups cake flour
>
> 2 teaspoons baking powder
>
> ¾ teaspoon baking soda
>
> 1½ teaspoons ground nutmeg
>
> 1½ teaspoons ground cinnamon
>
> ¾ teaspoon ground cloves
>
> ¾ teaspoon salt

At low speed, add the dry ingredients to the butter mixture alternately with:

> 1¼ cups buttermilk

In a separate bowl, at medium-high speed, beat until foamy:

> 4 large egg whites

Slowly beat in:

> ½ cup sugar

Beat at high speed until the whites form stiff peaks. Fold the whites gently into the cake batter with a rubber spatula, blending just until incorporated.

Pour 3 cups of the batter into one prepared pan and the remaining batter into the other. Bake the less full pan for 20 to 25 minutes and the fuller pan for 30 to 35 minutes, or until a cake tester inserted into the center of the cake comes out clean. Cool the cakes on a wire rack for 15 to 20 minutes before turning them out of their pans.

Yield: 8 cups of batter

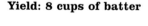

CHOCOLATE-HAZELNUT MOUSSE

A Bakehouse secret: All of our mousses are actually whipped cream with flavorings folded in. There are no egg whites to whip or egg yolks to fuss over. As you can see from the variations that follow, this is a very versatile filling that can be flavored almost any way you want. Spread a thin layer of your chosen flavoring directly on the cake layers before adding the filling to add moisture and enhance the flavor.

In the bowl of an electric mixer at high speed, whip until stiff:

   2 cups heavy cream

   4 tablespoons confectioners' sugar

   ½ teaspoon pure vanilla extract

Soften by heating in the microwave for 10 to 20 seconds or over a pan of hot water:

   ½ cup Nutella or other chocolate–hazelnut spread

Gently fold the Nutella into the whipped cream.

Yield: 4½ cups

Variations

RASPBERRY MOUSSE

Substitute ¼ raspberry purée for the Nutella; Williams-Sonoma carries one we like, but a fine raspberry jam will work, too. To use fresh raspberries, purée one quart of berries with 1 tablespoon of confectioners' sugar. Strain and use as above.

BAILEY'S IRISH CREAM MOUSSE

Substitute ¼ Bailey's Irish Cream for the Nutella. This is a grown-ups-only filling that goes very well with Freckled Mocha Cake (page 114).

COFFEE MOUSSE

Increase the confectioners' sugar to 6 tablespoons and substitute 2 tablespoons of instant espresso powder dissolved in 2 tablespoons of hot water for the Nutella.

Relief Chocolate Method

Though the basic forms for decorations made with the relief method are traced and filled on parchment as usual, the finishing touches are added freehand to the smooth surface once the form has hardened and been peeled off its parchment backing. This gives the pieces dimension and texture. You can take this even one step further, by making a design in segments, then reconstructing it in layers to create a three-dimensional object.

Feel free to limit the number of colors you use on your design; the important thing is to see the raised design against the smooth chocolate base.

What you will need:

Sheet pan or flat surface

Parchment paper

¼ cup dark wafer chocolate and 1 to 2 cups white wafer chocolate

7 small plastic bowls

Orange, pink, green, yellow, purple, and blue candy colors

Pastry cones

Rubber spatulas

How to:

1. Photocopy or trace the snowman template. Tape the template on a sheet pan or flat surface. Cover the template with parchment paper.

2. Separately melt the dark and white chocolate.

3. In the bowls, tint small amounts of the white chocolate light orange, yellow, blue, pink, purple, and green, leaving the bulk of the white for the body. Pour the tinted and dark chocolates into separate pastry cones.

4. Cut a small hole in the dark chocolate pastry cone. Pipe out the snowman's hat. Do not trace the snowman's outline.

5. Cut a large hole in the white pastry cone and pipe out three circles for the body, overlapping the hat to prevent breaking. Fill in the circles with more white chocolate. Set aside to harden.

6. When the chocolate has set, gently flip the design. Following the template for guidance if necessary, pipe a blue line to define the snowman's belly. Use the dark chocolate to pipe out coal eyes, mouth, and buttons. Use orange to pipe out a carrot nose, green to add a scarf, pink for the polka dots and fringe. Pipe a purple band around the hat with a yellow buckle. Add any other details you think might make the snowman come to life. Set aside until completely hardened.

Flowers

We think every baker should have one classically lovely confection in his or her repertoire, and this is probably one of the most traditional-looking cakes we make, with its densely clustered ring of flowers against a creamy white background. There is no reason, however, that you can't render this design in hotter colors or against a vividly hued icing. As always, the choice is yours. And if you love making buttercream roses—or want an excuse to try making them—this is your cake. The roses should be made in advance and frozen; the other types of flowers can be made ahead in the same manner or they can be piped directly onto the cake.

What you will need:

Cake: one 9-inch round cake (we recommend Carrot Cake, next page)

Icing: Cream Cheese Frosting (next page)

Decoration: Kaye's Buttercream (page 37) or House Buttercream (page 36), to make 12 to 15 buttercream roses and 8 to 20 buttercream pansies, blossoms, and/or chrysanthemums

Colors: violet, yellow, orange, and bright purple liquid gel colors

Tips: #104, #103, or #102 petal tip, #79 or #81 mum tip, and #125 rose tip

Rose nail

Ground nuts

How to:

1. Prepare a half batch of buttercream for the flowers and leaves. Set aside 1 cup of uncolored buttercream. Make the roses in a variety of colors, and freeze them, reserving the remaining buttercream for final decorations (see pages 107–109).

2. Bake the cake and let it cool completely. Prepare the icing. Fill and crumb coat the cake with Cream Cheese Frosting as directed on pages 30–32. Chill the filled cake.

3. Ice the cake with Cream Cheese Frosting. Press ground nuts around the bottom edge, then adhere the cardboard round supporting the cake to your base.

4. Place the reserved uncolored buttercream in a pastry bag with a coupler, and without a tip pipe a ring around the edge of the cake. Arrange the frozen roses onto the ring. Fill in the empty spaces with premade buds, mums, pansies, and blossoms, or pipe them directly onto the cake. Fill in the remaining spaces with leaves.

CARROT CAKE

Thirty years ago, when I lived on Nantucket, a friend gave me her recipe for carrot cake. I worked on it a bit and came up with this straightforward recipe, rich in nuts and raisins. Since I consider myself a chocolate lover at heart, I'm always surprised at how delicious I find this cake. When we made it for a friend's wedding, the guests demanded seconds.

Grease and flour two 9 × 3-inch round pans. Preheat the oven to 350° F. Have all ingredients at room temperature.

In the bowl of an electric mixer, beat at high speed until light and fluffy:

> **4 large eggs**
>
> **1½ cups oil**
>
> **2 cups sugar**

On a piece of wax paper, sift together:

> **2 cups all-purpose flour**
>
> **2 teaspoons baking soda**
>
> **2 teaspoons ground cinnamon**
>
> **1 teaspoon salt**

Add the dry ingredients to the batter at low speed and mix just until 75 percent incorporated, then add:

> **3 cups grated carrots**
>
> **1 cup coarsely chopped walnuts**
>
> **1 cup raisins**

Mix just until smooth.

Divide the batter evenly between the two pans. Bake for 35 to 40 minutes, or until a cake tester inserted into the center of each cake comes out clean. Cool the cakes on a wire rack for 15 to 20 minutes before turning them out of their pans.

Yield: 8 cups of batter

CREAM CHEESE FROSTING

Cream cheese frosting made with a little butter has the best flavor, texture, and creaminess. A bit of lemon juice keeps it from being overly sweet.

In the bowl of an electric mixer at medium-high speed, beat until creamy:

> **4 ounces (1 stick) unsalted butter**

Add and cream:

> **9 ounces cream cheese (three 3-ounce packages)**

Add all at once and beat at low speed until smooth:

> **6 cups sifted confectioners' sugar**
>
> **2 teaspoons fresh lemon juice**
>
> **1 teaspoon pure vanilla extract**

Continue to beat at medium speed until light and fluffy.

Yield: 2 cups frosting, enough to fill and ice a 9-inch cake

Buttercream Flowers

Some people find the process of piping flowers a bit intimidating. If you are among them, I offer the following words of wisdom: be loose. A well-decorated cake is not unlike an impressionist painting. Up close the brushstrokes (or in the case of a cake the dabs of buttercream) seem random and disembodied. Take a step back and they come together in a fusion of color and strokes to create a vibrant image. So if you are unhappy with an individual petal, try to see the flower as a whole. It may be more pleasing than you had imagined.

Choose a color palette that is appropriate to the occasion. In general I prefer soft and muted colors, but a jolt of neon can be a refreshing change.

For best results, make certain your buttercream has a firm consistency so the petals will hold their shape. All of the flowers with the exception of the rose use standard tips with a pastry bag and coupler. For larger roses no coupler is used; simply put the tip into the pastry bag before filling it with buttercream

The following are some of the flowers we use most frequently at the Bakehouse. The roses are the only flowers I make ahead of time and store in the freezer. All the rest are made directly on the cake. If you prefer, however, any of these can be made on a nail and frozen just like the roses, filling in with leaves and stems when you assemble the cake. If you have leftover tinted buttercream, why not pipe out a few extra flowers to keep in the freezer to pop onto a cupcake or cake for an everynight celebration?

DAISIES, CONEFLOWERS, AND BLACK-EYED SUSANS
Petal tip and round tip (#104 and #5)

FULL FLOWER

1. Choose a center point for the flower. Starting at the outer edge of each petal, squeeze, then release the pressure as you move in toward the center point.

2. Make four or five more petals in the same way, fanning out in a circle from the center point.

3. With a round tip, pipe a center dot.

PERSPECTIVE FLOWER

To make the flower in perspective, use the same piping technique, but pipe the petals in a semicircle. Pipe the dot on the top.

CHRYSANTHEMUMS
Mum tip (#79 or #81)

1. Holding the curved end of the tip down, pipe a row of petals in a ¾-inch circle. To pipe a petal, pull the tip up at a 30-degree angle and away from the center. Each petal should be approximately ½ to ⅓ inch long.

2. Pipe another row inside the first, overlapping the petals of the first row about halfway. For each progressive row increase the angle of the petals. Repeat this for each row until you reach the center. Finish by filling in the center with petals as needed.

ROSES

Petal tip (#125 for large roses, #104 for petite roses)

1. Using a dab of icing, stick a small square of parchment paper to a flower nail. If you are right-handed, hold the nail between the thumb and fingers of your left hand. Spin the nail clockwise and counterclockwise to get used to the movement.

2. Pipe a tight center for the rose by placing the wide end of the tip on the nail angling it slightly toward the center. Squeeze the bag and spin the nail clockwise simultaneously. The wide end of the tip should trace a small circle in the center of the nail. When your bud has completed one rotation, stop squeezing and drag the tip downward, overlapping the beginning of the bud.

3. Pipe another petal around the bud in the same manner, this time holding the tip almost vertical.

4. The next row has three petals. The tip should still rest on the nail, but flare it slightly from the previous row. Turning the nail in a counterclockwise direction, pipe the three petals, each petal touching the previous one.

5. The last row has five petals. The rose tip still rests on the nail and the petals should touch the previous row of petals. Flare the narrow end of the tip outward from the previous row, at approximately a 45-degree angle from the nail. Turn the nail counterclockwise. Each petal should overlap the previous one. To make the petal flare more, squeeze a little more at the center of each petal, and pull the tip upward slightly. The last petal should overlap the first. Carefully remove the rose by holding the parchment paper square. Place it on a sheet pan or flat surface. Freeze.

BLOSSOMS

Petal tip (#104)

The blossom is the foundation of the violet, apple blossom, wild rose, and daffodil. See below for the specific finishing details for each.

1. Choose a center point for the flower. You will need five evenly spaced petals of equal size. Place the wide end of the tip at the center point. The narrow end of the tip should be at a 30-degree angle to the cake.

2. Pivoting the tip around the center point, pipe the first petal by increasing pressure as you move the tip around. The curvature of the petal occurs not from moving the tip up and back toward the center point, but from increasing the pressure toward the middle of each petal. To finish each petal, drag the tip toward the center as you release the pressure. The wide end of the tip should remain close to the center.

3. Begin the next petal, so that it slightly overlaps the first. Repeat for each petal.

DAFFODILS

With yellow, orange, or white buttercream, pipe a circle in the center of the flower. Continue this circle, spiraling upwards, to make a cylinder.

VIOLETS

With yellow buttercream, pipe two dots in the center.

BLOSSOMS OR WILD ROSES

With yellow or orange buttercream, pipe a grouping of dots in the center.

PANSY

Petal tip (#104)

Pansies are formed with the same motions used to make a blossom, but using two colors.

1. With the first color, pipe one large petal, then two small but equal-size petals overlapping it.

2. With the second color, pipe two small petals opposite the first three.

3. To variegate the petals, place a small amount of each color in two pastry cones. Starting from the center of the petals, pipe thin lines in the contrasting color of the petal about one quarter of the way to halfway up the petal. Pipe a small circle in the center of the flower with the darker color.

BUDS

Petal tip (#104)

1. Hold the pastry bag with the wide end of the tip down and the narrow end at a 30-degree angle to the cake surface. Squeeze and pull the tip up and then down to the left as you release the pressure. The petal should overlap itself slightly.

2. Start the next petal slightly lower than your initial starting spot. Squeeze and pull down to the right.

3. Start the last petal flush with the right side of the bud in line with the starting point. Pull down to the left, overlapping the second petal.

Coffee Cup Cake

Every bit of this three-dimensional cake is completely edible—
even the spoon! Wouldn't it be a perfect treat for a tea party?
Because it is baked in a bowl there is no carving involved,
making it an ideal shaped cake for beginners. You can
customize your coffee cups by choosing any colored buttercream or pattern. Simply match the handle to the color of the
icing. Serve the cake with a biscotti or two to further heighten
the illusion.

What you will need:

Cake: three 6-inch round cakes and three 6-inch bowl cakes (we recommend Freckled Mocha Cake, page 114)

Icing: Kaye's Coffee Buttercream (page 38) and ½ recipe Chocolate Glaze (page 39)

Decoration: 2 cups dark wafer chocolate (white wafer chocolate is optional) to make 3 chocolate spoons and 3 chocolate handles (if desired, reserve ¼ cup of chocolate for decorative piping on the cup).

1 recipe Almond Biscotti (page 115)

Optional colors: yellow, green, pink, purple, blue liquid gel colors.

Tips: #44 flat tip (a #46 or #47 basket weave can be substituted) and #4 or #7 round tip

1 tablespoon instant espresso powder

Cellophane sheets

Silver luster dust

How to:

1. Make 6 cups of cake batter. Grease three 6-inch round pans and three 6-inch stainless-steel bowls. Pour 1 cup of batter into each 6-inch pan and 1 cup of batter into each 6-inch bowl. Bake for 20 to 25 minutes. Cool completely on a wire rack, then turn the cakes out of their pans.

2. Prepare the coffee buttercream.

3. Make 6 spoons and handles using the One-Color Chocolate Method (page 54). For a more realistic look, brush the spoons with silver luster dust, and highlight with a piped dark chocolate pattern.

4. Cut one round cake in half horizontally and place both layers on a 6-inch cardboard round. Invert one domed cake on top. Trim the bowl flush with the round cakes. Trim a small amount of cake off the top to level the bowl (this creates a flat, stable base for when the cake is flipped). Repeat with the remaining round and domed cakes.

5. Fill the cakes with thin layers of coffee buttercream (do not ring); the domed cakes are on top. Crumb coat the cakes (see pages 30–32). To smooth buttercream, hold a 2 × 10-inch strip of cellophane at both ends and drag it over the cake starting at the bottom. Continue around the circumference of the cake until it is smooth. The cellophane will curve to the shape of the cake, unlike a metal spatula. Chill the filled cake.

6. Finish the cakes with coffee buttercream, again using the cellophane to smooth the buttercream. The tops should have only a scraping of buttercream.

7. If you like, fill a pastry cone with some of the leftover melted dark chocolate or colored coffee buttercream and pipe a pattern on each cake. The photograph can be your guide, or you can make up your own design.

8. Hold the cake in your hand and carefully place a covered cardboard round or base onto the top of the domed cake. Steady the plate with one hand and the cake with the other hand and invert. The coffee cup should now be right side up in the center of the base. Repeat with the remaining cakes.

9. Mark the side of each cake where the handle will go. Insert a knife at these two marks, to ease the entrance of the handle. Push the handles in.

10. Remove the top 6-inch cardboard round from the cake and spread a thin layer of coffee buttercream on the cake surface. Place the remaining coffee buttercream in a pastry bag with a coupler, and with a round tip pipe a circle around the top edge. This will be the reservoir for the "coffee." Repeat for each remaining cake.

11. Change to a flat tip and pipe a lip on the coffee cup, covering the circle piped around the top edge. If desired, pipe coffee buttercream dots or lines on the handle to match the cup's patterns. Stick the spoons and biscotti onto the plates with dabs of buttercream. Repeat for each remaining cake.

12. Chill the cakes until the buttercream has set.

13. Combine ¾ cup melted chocolate glaze with 1 tablespoon espresso powder mixed with 1 teaspoon hot water. Fill each cup's reservoir with the icing without going over the edge.

FRECKLED MOCHA CAKE

The divine combination of chocolate and coffee put the idea for this cake in motion. It has a subtle coffee flavor and is filled with flecks of grated chocolate. It marries well with chocolate mousse, coffee mousse, or my favorite, Bailey's Irish Cream Mousse (page 100). You can bake it in anything from a baking sheet to a bowl, as we do for the Coffee Cup Cakes.

Grease two 8 × 3-inch round pans. Preheat the oven to 350°F. Have all ingredients at room temperature.

In the bowl of an electric mixer, beat at high speed until light and fluffy:

> 6 ounces (1½ sticks) unsalted butter
>
> 1½ cups sugar

Add at medium speed and beat well:

> 4 extra-large egg yolks
>
> 1 teaspoon pure vanilla extract

On a piece of wax paper, sift together:

> 2½ cups cake flour
>
> 1½ teaspoons baking powder
>
> ½ teaspoon salt

In a separate bowl dissolve:

> 1 tablespoon plus ¼ teaspoon instant espresso powder
>
> ¼ cup hot water

Add:

> ¾ cup milk

Add the dry ingredients to the butter and egg mixture alternately with the coffee-flavored milk, beating at medium-low speed until the batter is smooth.

Fold in by hand:

> 1½ ounces grated semisweet chocolate

Pour 2 cups of batter into one prepared pan and the remaining batter into the other. Bake the less full pan for 18 to 25 minutes and the fuller pan for 20 to 30 minutes, or until a cake tester inserted into the center of the cake comes out clean. Cool the cakes on a wire rack for 15 to 20 minutes before turning them out of the pans.

Yield: 6 cups of batter

ALMOND BISCOTTI

This basic biscotti recipe adds the finishing touch to our Coffee Cup Cake. If you like anise seeds, as I do, by all means add them but be aware that they add a very distinct taste. Leftovers are the perfect accompaniment to a real cup of coffee.

Line a cookie sheet with parchment paper. Preheat the oven to 325°F. Have all ingredients at room temperature.

In the bowl of an electric mixer, beat at medium speed until light and fluffy:

> 3 ounces (¾ stick) unsalted butter
>
> ½ teaspoon salt
>
> ½ cup brown sugar, firmly packed

Mix in at medium speed:

> 2 extra-large eggs
>
> ½ teaspoon pure almond extract

On a piece of wax paper, sift together:

> 1¾ cups all-purpose flour
>
> ¾ teaspoon baking powder

Add:

> ¾ cup whole toasted almonds (see Note)

Add the dry ingredients and almonds to the butter and egg mixture and combine quickly. Do not overmix. Transfer from the bowl to a work surface, knead briefly, then form into a 7-inch log. Place the log on the cookie sheet. Press on the log with your hand to flatten it to 4 inches in width. Bake for 1 hour to 1 hour and 15 minutes, or until golden brown. Cool completely. Lower the oven temperature to 300°F. Slice the cookie log into ¾-inch pieces with a serrated knife. Place the biscotti on the cookie sheet lined with fresh parchment paper. Bake for an additional hour and 15 minutes, turning as needed to ensure golden brown color on both sides.

Note: Toast the unskinned almonds on an ungreased cookie sheet for 10 to 15 minutes at 350°F.

part three
TIERED CAKES

There's something about a tiered cake that's a bit more special than the fanciest layer cake. Even when the tiers are small, people stop and take notice of a cake with two or more graduated tiers, and unlike a sheet cake, a stacked cake definitely makes a statement. While tiered cakes are expected at a wedding, there's no reason they can't be made for birthdays, holidays, showers—you name it.

Another advantage of a multiple tiered cake is the opportunity it affords for telling a story, with each tier serving as a separate chapter in the unfolding tale. Even if you're not creating a pictorial cake, the design opportunities are myriad: you may want to treat each tier the same for a more unified, yet still impressive, effect, or allow each tier to express its own point of view. If you've mastered the art of assembling tilted layers, you'll find the offbeat effect is even more striking on a multi-tiered cake, making it especially suitable for a child's party or one at which a hint of eccentricity would be welcome.

We often employ two or more different decorating techniques on a tiered cake, perhaps adding piped embellishments to one tier and placing chocolate ornaments on the upper tier. And you can really go wild by varying the flavors of the cakes and fillings in each layer. All of the recipes, with the exception of the cheesecakes and Truffle Cake, can be used for the cakes illustrated here. Try one tier of Freckled Mocha Cake filled with Coffee Mousse, topped with another tier of Golden Butter Cake filled with French Custard. Or combine two cakes in one—maybe two layers of Hazelnut Cake and one layer of Chocolate Butter Cake, filled with Chocolate-Hazelnut Mousse. Try two fillings in one cake; Lemon and Raspberry Mousse with White Butter Cake, for example. And don't feel limited by our suggestions.

Assembling Tiered Cakes

We don't much care for the airy, see-through effect of cake tiers perching on fluted columns; all our tiered cakes are stacked one on top of the other. This makes for cakes that are less risky to transport and a bit more down-to-earth. It is also more in keeping with our philosophy that the less inedible material on a cake, the better.

Decide before you start if you want your cake level or tilted. The level foundation is just that, a foundation; color, piping, and chocolate designs play an equal or more important role in setting the mood of a cake. However, if you are looking to go over-the-top, tilting the tiers creates a kinetic feeling that heightens the effect of any whimsical design.

- Putting together a tiered cake is not really much more complicated than making any other cake. In fact, if you think of it as making two (or three or more) individual cakes, then stacking them one on top of the other, it is far less intimidating. The cakes can be of almost any size, but each tier should be at least 2 inches larger in diameter than the one above it. Because the weight of the upper tiers would cause the lowest tier to collapse, you must introduce a structural support element. We use wooden dowels, but if your cake is quite small, plastic drinking straws will also work. Be sure to use a sturdy base; cardboard will not be rigid enough to hold any but the smallest tiered cakes.

- To serve a tiered cake, cut the top tier as you would a single-layer cake. To get a clean slice, dip your sharp knife in hot water, dry it off, and cut. Repeat this whenever the knife gets cool, or messy. When you have finished cutting and serving the top tier, remove the cardboard round it was supported by. The dowels from the cake below should be visible. Remove all of the dowels and cut the cake as you did the top tier. For cakes larger than 10 inches, cut a circle 2 to 3 inches from the edge, then cut slices around this circle. For cakes 12 inches or larger, you may need to cut two or more concentric circles.

What you will need:

- Cake: 2 or 3 cakes of your choice differing by at least 2 inches in diameter

- Filling: your choice of filling

- Icing: your choice of icing

- Foil- or fabric-covered wooden board at least 4 inches larger than the bottom tier (wood is recommended, but any solid, inflexible material can be substituted, such as ½-inch-thick Plexiglas)

- Cardboard cake rounds of the same diameters as the cakes

- ⅛- to ¼-inch dowels (straws can be substituted for small tiered cakes)

- Pruning shears for cutting dowels

Level Tiered Cakes

1. Bake the cakes and cool completely. Prepare the filling and icing. Fill and crumb coat each individual cake as directed on pages 30–32. Chill the filled cakes.

2. Ice the largest tier. Glue the cardboard round supporting the bottom or largest tier to the center of your base.

3. Most tiered cakes are stacked along a central axis. In the center of the bottom tier place a cardboard round the same size as the cake to be stacked on top, and with a toothpick trace the circumference. Carefully remove the cardboard round. Press a dowel all the way into the center of the cake. Mark the dowel at the buttercream line with a pencil or hold it with your finger. Remove the dowel and cut it $\frac{1}{16}$ inch shorter than that line. Using this dowel as a guide, cut 6 to 8 more dowels to the same length. (You will need the following numbers of dowels per tier, depending on the size and number of tiers stacked on top: 3 for a 4-inch cake, 3 to 4 for a 6-inch cake, 4 to 6 for an 8-inch cake, 5 to 7 for a 9-inch cake, 6 to 8 for a 10-inch cake, 8 to 12 for a 12-inch cake, 10 to 14 for a 14-inch cake, and so on.) Insert the dowels into the cake, placing one dowel in the center, and the remaining dowels in a circle around it all within the demarcation. Pipe a small dot of buttercream on top of each dowel.

4. Ice the second tier and center it on top of the bottom tier, using the line you drew as a guide. Trace a cardboard cake round the same size as the cake to be stacked on top, and insert the dowels to support the top tier.

5. Ice the top tier and center it on top of the middle tier, using the line you drew as a guide.

6. If you are traveling with the cake or want added stability, sharpen one end of a dowel the height of the finished cake and carefully hammer it through all of the cakes and cardboard rounds to the base.

Tilted Tiered Cakes

Tilted cakes are put together much the same way as their more levelheaded cousins, but the dowels must be individually measured as each will be a different height. To serve a tilted cake, cut the top tier as you would a level tiered cake. When you have finished cutting and serving the top tier, remove the dowel that runs through the entire cake, then remove the cardboard round the top tier was supported by. Continue cutting the remaining cake as you would a level tiered cake.

1. Bake the cakes and let them cool completely. Prepare the icing and filling. Fill and crumb coat each individual cake as directed in Filling a Tilted Cake (page 33). Chill.

2. Ice the largest tier. Glue the cardboard circle supporting the bottom or largest tier to the center of your base.

3. In the center of the bottom tier place a cardboard cake round the same size as the cake to be stacked on top and with a toothpick mark the circumference. Carefully remove the cake round without disturbing the buttercream. Within this demarcation, each dowel must be pressed into the cake separately. Mark each dowel at the buttercream line with a pencil or hold it with your finger. Remove each dowel and cut it $1/16$ inch shorter than that line, using pruning shears. Stick each cut dowel back into its initial hole. Do not place a dowel in the center. (You will need from 3 to 8 or more dowels, depending on the cake size; see the preceding page.) Pipe a small dot of buttercream on top of each dowel.

4. Ice the second tier and center it on top of the bottom tier, with the lowest point of the second tier in line with the highest point of the bottom tier. In the center of the middle tier place a cardboard cake round the same size as the cake to be stacked on top and with a toothpick mark the circumference. Carefully remove the cake round without disturbing the buttercream. Insert the dowels to support the top tier.

5. Ice the second tier and center it on top of the middle tier, with the lowest point of the top tier in line with the highest point of the middle tier.

6. Sharpen one end of a dowel the height of the finished cake and carefully hammer it through the center of all of the cakes and cardboard rounds to the base. This will stabilize the stacked layers and prevent slipping.

White on White

Perfectly simple, this charming cake is a wonderful example of how a minimalist design can make as strong an impression as one that pulls out all the stops. If you want to make a more formal cake but don't have perfect piping skills yet, this design fits the bill; the tone-on-tone chocolate decorations have a subtle look that is similar to traditional piping effects. Because the chocolate ornaments aren't colored, these are simplicity itself to make.

Techniques used to make this cake: Assembling Tiered Cakes (page 119), One-Color Chocolate Method (page 54), and Piping (page 66).

What you will need:

Cake: 3 tiers, including one 10-inch round cake, one 8-inch round cake, and one 6-inch round cake; 16 cups batter for Hazelnut Cake (page 73)

Filling: 11 cups Chocolate–Hazelnut Mousse (page 100)

Icing: 1½ to 2 recipes Kaye's Buttercream (page 37) or House Buttercream (page 36)

Decoration: 2 cups white wafer chocolate to make 30 swirls and 80 to 90 polka dots

Tips: #104, #103, or #102 petal tip, a #4 or #5 round tip, and a #44 flat tip (a #46 or #47 can be substituted)

How to:

1. Melt 2 cups of white wafer chocolate. Pipe out 30 white wafer chocolate swirls and 80 to 90 small polka dots using the One-Color Chocolate Method (page 54). Set aside to harden.

2. Bake the cakes and let them cool completely. Prepare the icing and filling. Fill and crumb coat the cakes as illustrated in "The Basics of Cake Assembly" (page 28). Chill the filled cakes.

3. Ice the bottom (10-inch) tier with buttercream. Place 1½ cups of buttercream in a pastry bag with a coupler, and alternating between a round and flat tip, pipe a plaid pattern over the entire surface, as illustrated on page 69. Glue the cardboard circle supporting the cake to your base. Insert dowels to support the next tier.

4. Ice the middle (8-inch) tier with the buttercream and before it sets, press on the spirals. Center the cake on top of the bottom tier. Insert dowels to support the top tier.

5. Ice the top (6-inch) tier with buttercream and before it sets, press the polka dots onto the sides and top in an evenly spaced pattern. Center the cake on top of the second tier.

6. Change to a petal tip and pipe a Flat Ribbon Border (page 68) around the base of the bottom tier. With a round tip, pipe a Crazy Border (page 67) around the base of the second tier and a Bead Border (page 67) around the base of the top tier.

Summer Daze

This cake evokes everything we love about summer: the clouds as they change shapes, the gorgeous flowers that fill the garden, and the languid breeze on a sunny July afternoon. Hot, clear colors seem to suit the subject matter best, and the tilted assembly gives the cake a casual look that is in keeping with summer's more informal entertaining. This cake incorporates both applied and piped decorations; the simpler dots on the middle tier help to unify the cake and provide a transition from tier to tier.

Techniques used to make this cake: Tilted Tiered Cake (page 121), One-Color Chocolate Method (page 54), Advanced Chocolate Method (page 93), and Piping (page 66).

What you will need:

Cake: 3 tiers, including: one 10-inch round cake, one 8-inch round cake, and one 6-inch round cake; 16 cups batter for Golden Butter Cake (page 91)

Filling: 11 cups Whipped Chocolate Ganache (page 60)

Icing: 2 recipes Kaye's Buttercream (page 37) or House Buttercream (page 36)

Decoration: 1 cup dark wafer chocolate and 5½ cups white wafer chocolate to make 1 sun's face with 6 pointed rays, 3 small rays, and 6 swirled rays; 10 clouds; 12 coneflowers with leaves and stems; 12 daisies with leaves and stems; and 30 polka dots

Colors: liquid gel colors in sky blue, neon purple, neon pink, and yellow candy colors in blue, red, yellow, green, purple, pink, and orange

Tips: #104 and #102 petal tip, #44 flat tip (#46 or #47 can be substituted), and #2 and #5, #6, or #7 round tip

How to:

1. Melt 1 cup of dark wafer chocolate and 5½ cups of white wafer chocolate. Set aside ½ cup of white chocolate for the clouds. Using the Color Mixing Chart on page 26, tint the remaining white chocolate; approximately ½ cup red-orange, ½ cup orange, 1 cup yellow, ½ cup lime green, ½ cup leaf green, ½ cup sky blue, ½ cup neon pink, and 1 cup pink-purple. Using the templates provided, make 10 clouds; 1 sun's face; 6 swirled rays; 6 large and 3 small pointed rays; 6 coneflowers; 6 perspective coneflowers; and 12 daisies, stems, and leaves as illustrated in the Advanced Chocolate Method (page 93). Pipe out polka dots with the extra colored chocolate. Set aside to harden.

2. Bake the cakes and let them cool completely. Prepare the filling and icing. Fill and crumb coat the cakes as directed in Filling a Tilted Cake (page 32). Chill the filled cakes.

3. Set aside 1 cup of uncolored buttercream. Prepare the colored buttercream: approximately 2 cups sky blue, ½ cup lime green, 3 cups yellow, 4 cups pink, 1 cup fuchsia.

4. Ice the bottom tier with pink buttercream. Place the fuchsia buttercream into a pastry bag with a coupler, and with a flat tip, pipe lattice over the entire surface. Glue the cardboard circle supporting the cake to the center of your base. Insert dowels to support the next tier.

5. Ice the middle tier with yellow buttercream. Add a few more drops of yellow color to the remaining yellow buttercream and place it in a pastry bag with a coupler, and with a small round tip, pipe Crazy Curls (page 67) over the entire surface. Center the middle tier on top of the bottom tier. Insert dowels to support the top tier.

6. Ice the top tier with the sky blue. Fill a pastry cone with white buttercream and cut a small hole. Pipe free-hand linear clouds in white. Center the top tier on top of the middle tier. Sharpen one end of a dowel the height of the finished cake and carefully hammer it through the center of all the cakes and cardboard rounds to the base.

7. With a petal tip, pipe a fuchsia Crazy Border (page 68) around the bottom tier. Place the reserved white buttercream in a pastry bag with a coupler, and with a round tip, pipe a Cloud Border (page 68) below the Crazy Border. With the same tip, pipe a Cloud Border around the top tier. With a round tip, pipe a yellow Crazy Curl border around the middle tier.

8. Before the buttercream sets, adhere the stems, flowers, and leaves randomly around the sides of the bottom tier. If they won't stay in place use little dabs of buttercream to adhere the designs.

9. Choose a front for the cake that best shows off the tilt and the top tier. Arrange the pointed rays equidistant from each other on the top tier. The tips should extend over the edge by at least 1 inch. Pipe a small dot of sky-blue buttercream between each ray. Apply the swirled rays to the dots. Pipe a large dot of buttercream in the middle of the rays and press the sun in place. Tilt it toward the front of the cake by pressing gently on the bottom edge.

10. Randomly space the clouds around the sides of the top tier using a bit of buttercream to adhere them. Press the polka dots onto the middle tier to unify the cake.

New York, New York

Many artists have tried to capture the hustle and bustle of city life; this is our edible paean to the Big Apple and it has all the energy and excitement of a night out on the town. Although this cake boasts only two tiers, each is densely packed with such architectural icons as the Brooklyn Bridge, the Statue of Liberty, and the Empire State Building, all depicted against a glowing night sky. Try substituting landmarks from your own hometown or a place that is special to the guest of honor. This would look just as great with a bold Eiffel Tower or Space Needle embellishment!

Techniques used to make this cake: Tilted Tiered Cakes (page 121), Relief Chocolate Method (page 101), Variegated Icing, and Piping (page 66).

What you will need:

Cake: 2 tiers, including: one 9-inch round cake and one 6-inch round cake; 9 cups batter for Freckled Mocha Cake (page 114)

Filling: 7¼ cups Bailey's Irish Cream Mousse (page 100)

Icing: 1 to 1½ recipes Kaye's Buttercream (page 37) or House Buttercream (page 36)

Decoration: 2 cups dark wafer chocolate and 8 cups white wafer chocolate to make a Brooklyn Bridge, Statue of Liberty, Chrysler Building, Empire State Building, Guggenheim Museum, Central Park Lake, and 10 to 12 miscellaneous buildings, 7 taxis, 10 people, and 3 trees

Colors: liquid gel colors in sky blue, royal blue, teal, purple, green, and yellow; candy colors in sky blue, yellow, green, purple, yellow, pink, blue, and orange

¼ cup clear piping gel

Tips: #104, #103, or #102 petal tip

How to:

1. Melt 2 cups dark wafer chocolate and 8 cups white wafer chocolate. Set aside ½ cup of the white chocolate for highlights. Using the Color Mixing Chart on page 26, tint the remaining white chocolate: approximately 3 cups sky blue, ½ cup lime green, 1 cup yellow, ½ cup violet, ½ cup midnight blue, ½ cup orange, ½ cup pink, ½ cup peach, ¼ cup brown, and ½ cup green. Make the buildings, the Statue of Liberty, people, trees, and taxis using the Relief Chocolate Method (page 101). To create the curved contour of the bridge, tape the template and parchment paper onto the inside (concave) curve of a 9-inch round cake pan. Trace and fill as usual, then set aside to harden. When the

chocolate is set, peel off the template and decorate the smooth outside surface using the relief method. The finished decoration will then curve around the cake. When the white chocolate lake is hardened peel off the parchment and spread a thin layer of aqua-tinted piping gel on the smooth surface.

2. Bake the cakes and let them cool completely. Prepare the filling and icing. Fill and crumb coat the cakes as directed in Filling a Tilted Cake (page 33). Chill the filled cakes.

3. Prepare the colored buttercream; 2½ cups midnight blue, 1½ cups dark purple, 3 cups teal, 1½ cup light yellow, and ¼ cup orange.

4. Ice the bottom tier with a variegated finish. Spread a 1-inch band of teal buttercream around the base of the cake. Spread a ½-inch band of light yellow above the teal. Cover the remainder of the cake with midnight blue. Dip a flat metal spatula or scraper into hot water, wipe it dry, then, while spinning the turntable, run the heated scraper or spatula around the side of the cake using the cardboard round as your guide. The blue, yellow, and green will blend into each other.

5. Glue the cardboard circle supporting the cake to the center of your base. Insert dowels to support the top tier.

6. Ice the top tier with a variegated dark purple and midnight blue. Center the top tier on top of the bottom tier. Sharpen one end of a dowel the height of the finished cake and carefully hammer it through the center of all of the cakes and cardboard rounds to the base.

7. Choose a front for the cake. Mark where each building will be placed and score the cake with a small knife at these points. Carefully press the buildings about ½ inch into the cake. Arrange the taxis in front, securing them with a bit of buttercream. Score the sides of the bottom tier as above and press the buildings and Statue of Liberty into place at an angle. Press the bridge around the side of the cake and arrange the taxis on the bridge, adhering them with a bit of buttercream.

8. Put the remaining teal buttercream into a pastry bag with a coupler, and with a petal tip, pipe a Crazy Border (page 67) around the base to simulate the East River. With the same tip, around the base of the top tier, pipe a sidewalk that weaves among the buildings. Fill pastry cones with yellow and orange buttercream and pipe out dots for stars.

9. Set the lake in place on top and arrange a cluster of trees behind it and the people in front.

Autumn Harvest

This pear motif was borrowed from a wedding cake we made
for an October wedding set in the hills of upstate New York.
Pears were printed on the bride's invitations and nestled in
her floral centerpieces. This cake also shows how effective
combining a variety of cake shapes and sizes can be;
this is equally alluring from any side. The garland of
robustly colored flowers around the base is a gorgeous
way to embellish any cake, even a single-tiered one.
If you are looking for a cake that is a little less
lavish, try decorating an entire cake with the
bright blades of wheat grass that adorn the
topmost tier. I think you will be pleased.
Techniques used to make this cake:
Assembling Tiered Cakes (page 119), the
One-Color Chocolate Method (page 54), the
Advanced Chocolate Method (page 93), and
Piping (page 66).

What you will need:

Cake: 3 tiers, including one 15-inch hexagonal cake, one 8-inch square cake, and one 6-inch round cake; 20 cups batter for Hazelnut Cake (page 73) or Spice Cake (page 99)

Filling: 18 cups Chocolate-Hazelnut Mousse (page 100) for Hazelnut Cake or French Custard (page 87) for Spice Cake

Icing: 3 to 4 recipes Kaye's Buttercream (page 37) or House Buttercream (page 36). Reserve half of a recipe for making roses.

Decoration: 1½ cups dark wafer chocolate and 9 cups white wafer chocolate to make 1 chocolate sunflower with leaves (see page 94), 22 small and 10 large chocolate pears and leaves; 36 buttercream roses (see page 108)

Colors: burgundy, violet, bright purple, green, orange, brown, and yellow liquid gel colors and Yellow, green, red, and orange candy colors

Tips: #104, #103, or #102 petal tips and # 2, #4 and #7 round tips

How to:

1. Melt 1½ cups dark wafer chocolate and 9 cups white wafer chocolate. Using the Color Mixing Chart on page 26, tint the white chocolate: approximately ½ cup red-orange, ½ cup orange, 1 cup yellow, 2 cups soft yellow, ½ cup light brown, 1 cup autumn green, 1 cup leaf green, 1 cup sage green, 1 cup dark sage green, and ½ cup lime green. Using the Advanced Chocolate Method, make the pears with leaves and sunflower with leaves. On a sheet pan lined with parchment paper, trace a horizontal line as a guide for the ground level of the grass. Pipe out chocolate grass in different shades of green, overlapping the blades. The grass can "grow" up to a height of 4 inches.

2. Tint the reserved buttercream for the roses. Place the rose tip in a bag and fill the bag with tinted buttercream. Using a rose nail, pipe out a variety of colored roses and freeze them. (See Buttercream Roses, page 108.) Set aside the extra colored buttercream for buds.

3. Bake the cakes and let them cool completely. Prepare the filling and icing. Fill and crumb coat the hexagonal and square cakes as directed in "The Basics of Cake Assembly" (pages 30–32). Tilt the top layer as directed in "Filling a Tilted Cake" (page 33). Chill the filled cakes.

4. Set aside 3 cups of uncolored buttercream. Prepare the colored buttercream: approximately 7 cups pale sage, 5 cups pale mauve, 1 cup light green, and 3 cups dark moss green.

5. Ice the bottom tier with pale sage-green buttercream. Place the moss-green buttercream in a pastry bag with a coupler, and with a small round tip, pipe curved stems on each side of the hexagon. Pipe small off-shoots from each stem. Glue the card-board supporting the cake to your base. Insert dowels to support the next tier.

6. Ice the second tier with pale mauve buttercream. Pipe moss-green thyme branches and offshoots at different heights on each side. Pipe small thyme leaves on the branches and floating all over the layer. The motion for piping the leaves is similar to forming a bead or a teardrop. Center the middle tier on top of the bottom tier. Insert the dowels to support the top tier.

7. Ice the top tier with the reserved white buttercream. Center the top tier on top of the middle tier.

8. Pipe a dot of buttercream on the back of each pear and adhere them to the bottom tier at the tip of each stem. Stick the smaller pears to the offshoots. Apply the chocolate leaves.

9. Remove the tip from the pastry bag filled with moss green and pipe a ring around the base of the bottom tier. Apply the pre-made, frozen roses to the ring. Place the leftover colors from the roses in a pastry bag with a coupler, and with a petal tip, fill in the spaces between the roses with buds. With a leaf tip pipe moss-green and light green leaves.

10. On the second tier pipe small thyme leaves in various sizes as a border.

11. Break the chocolate grass into workable segments and place them flush with the circumference of the top tier, adhering them with dabs of buttercream if necessary. Pipe buttercream blades of grass as filler.

12. Pipe a mound of buttercream on top of the cake and press the sunflower in place, tilting it toward the low point of the tier. Arrange the chocolate leaves around it.

Safari

Animals, whether those found on a farm, in a jungle, or in a wild game preserve, make a great theme for children's cakes. Here a rainbow-maned lion watches over his colorful kingdom from a high perch, as a veritable ark's worth of wildlife parades around the tiers below.

Techniques used to make this cake: Assembling Tiered Cakes (page 118) Multicolor Chocolate Method (page 78), Variegated Icing, and Piping (page 66).

What you will need:

Cake: 2 tiers, including one 9-inch round cake and one 6-inch round cake; 9 cups batter for Lemon Ginger Cream Cheese Pound Cake (page 59) or Chocolate Chip Pound Cake (page 58)

Filling: 5½ cups Lemon Mousse (page 61) for Lemon Ginger Pound Cake or Whipped Chocolate Ganache (page 60) for Chocolate Chip Pound Cake

Icing: 1½ recipes Kaye's Buttercream (page 37) or House Buttercream (page 36)

Decoration: 2 cups dark wafer chocolate and 8 cups white wafer chocolate to make 2 mirror-image chocolate lions, giraffes, elephants, zebras, and tigers; 1 each hippo, rhino, and leopard; and 4 trees

Colors: sky-blue, green, orange, and yellow liquid gel colors and blue, pink, yellow, green, purple, red, and orange candy colors

Tips: #104, #103, or #102 petal tip and #2, #4 and #7 round tips

How to:

1. Melt 2 cups dark wafer chocolate and 8 cups white wafer chocolate. Set aside 1 cup of uncolored white chocolate. Using the Color Mixing Chart on page 26, tint the remaining white chocolate: approximately ½ cup red, ½ cup royal blue, 1 cup orange, 2 cups yellow, ½ cup sky blue, 1 cup lavender, ½ cup pink, ½ cup lime green, and ½ cup leaf green. Trace two lions onto parchment paper. Turn one upside down, and one right side up. Place another sheet of parchment paper over them. Make the two lions as directed in the Multicolor Chocolate Method. Extend their legs 1 inch with chocolate. Using this technique, make one set of each animal. Extend the legs of one of each animal by ½ inch with chocolate. Make the trees.

2. Bake the cakes and let them cool completely. Prepare the filling and

icing. Fill and crumb coat the cakes as directed in The Basics of Cake Assembly (page 28). Chill the filled cakes.

3. Set aside ¼ cup of uncolored buttercream. Prepare the colored buttercream: approximately 2 cups lime green, 2 cups yellow, 2 cups sky blue, and 2 cups orange.

4. Ice the bottom tier with a variegated finish. Spread a 1-inch band of orange buttercream around the base of the cake. Spread a ½-inch band of yellow above the orange. Cover the remainder of the cake with lime green. Dip a flat metal spatula or scraper into hot water, wipe it dry, then, while spinning the turntable, run the heated scraper or spatula around the side of the cake using the cardboard round as your guide. The orange, yellow, and green will blend into each other.

5. Fill a pastry cone with lime-green

buttercream and pipe a line of grass around the middle of the cake. Glue the cardboard round supporting the cake to your base. Insert dowels to support the next tier.

6. Ice the second tier with variegated green and blue buttercream. Fill a pastry cone with the reserved white buttercream and pipe linear white clouds around the cake. Follow the directions for Assembling Tiered Cakes (page 118). However, place the top tier off-center on top of the bottom tier so there is more space for the animals.

7. Place the leftover orange buttercream in a pastry bag with a coupler, and with a petal tip, pipe a Crazy Border (page 67) around the bottom tier. Pipe a green Crazy Border around the top tier.

8. Mark the top of the bottom tier with the extended feet of the first set of animals. Score the cake with a knife at these points. Carefully press the animals into their corresponding points up to their feet. Adhere a couple of trees to the background. Adhere the second set of animals and a couple of trees to the side of the bottom tier. Some can overlap.

9. Lightly mark the position of the lions on the top tier with their legs. They should be centered with their backs facing each other. Stick a knife into the cake at these points. Carefully press the lions into the slots until their paws are resting on the icing. Fill in the empty spaces between them with piped confetti or flowers, using the leftover tinted buttercream.

Quilting Bee

Among her many other talents, my mom is a fabulous knitter and a gifted seamstress. Although she loves to tell how I could thread a needle by the age of three, my sewing skills don't hold a candle to hers. One of the first things she ever made me was a patchwork quilt that I cherished so much it became threadbare after years of use. I still miss it and am reminded of that quilt every time I "stitch" together one of these colorful, versatile cakes. Think of each plane of the hexagonally shaped cakes as a quilt block, and give each its own unique pattern for the liveliest look. It's a good opportunity to incorporate motifs that have a special meaning for you or the intended recipient and other guests without getting too corny about it.

Try changing the palette from pastel to bold, bright, and colorful; you will be amazed at the result.

Techniques used to make this cake: Assembling Tiered Cakes (page 118), One-Color Chocolate Method (page 54), Relief Chocolate Method (page 101), and Piping (page 66).

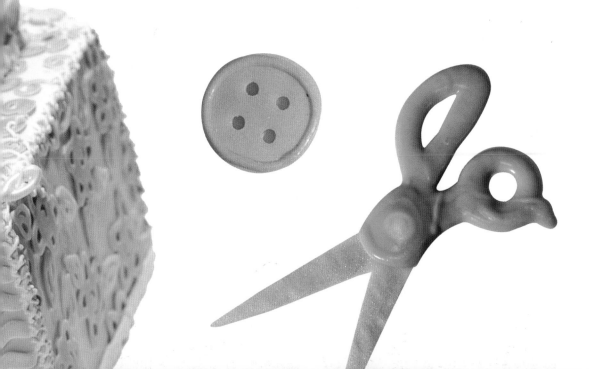

What you will need:

Cake: 3 cakes, including one 12-inch, one 9-inch, and one 6-inch hexagonal cake, made with 16 cups batter for Spice Cake (page 99)

Filling: 13 cups (3 recipes) French Custard (page 87)

Icing: 2 to 2½ recipes Kaye's Buttercream (page 37) or House Buttercream (page 36)

Decoration: 5 cups white wafer chocolate to make 1 each scissors and needle, 72 miscellaneous buttons, and 12 each polka dots, stars, roses, violets, and hearts

Colors: candy color in blue, green, pink, purple, yellow, and orange liquid gel in blue, green, pink, purple, yellow, and orange

Tips: #104, #103, or #102 petal tip; #44 flat tip (#46 or #47 can be substituted); and #2, #4, #7, and #10 round tips

2-inch and 2½-inch round cookie cutters

How to:

1. Melt 5 cups of white wafer chocolate. Set aside 1 cup of the white chocolate. Using the Color Mixing Chart on page 26, tint the remaining white chocolate: approximately ½ cup each of pale peach, pale yellow, pale lavender, pale pink, pale green, and pale blue. Using the One-Color Chocolate Method, make the buttons, needles, and fabric patterns (hearts, stars, rose, dots, etc.). Using the Relief Chocolate Method, make some buttons and the scissors.

2. Bake the cakes and let them cool completely. Prepare the filling and icing. Fill and crumb coat the cakes as directed in "The Basics of Cake Assembly" (page 28). Chill the filled cakes.

3. To make the spool's top and bottom pour a ¼-inch layer of melted white chocolate onto parchment paper, covering approximately a 5-inch square. When the chocolate is set but not completely hard, cut out two 2½-inch circles with the cookie cutter. Cut a hole in the center of each with a #10 round tip. Use a 2-inch cookie cutter to cut out two circles from the 6-inch cake. Stick them together with butter-cream. Ice the mini cake with a thin coat of buttercream. Press the spool top and bottom onto each end of the mini cake. Press a skewer through the center of the spool. Chill. When it is set, pipe melted colored chocolate around the spool by spinning the skewer in one hand and piping with the other.

4. Set aside 5 cups of uncolored buttercream. Prepare the colored buttercream: approximately 1½ cups each of pale blue, pale peach, pale yellow, pale lavender, pale pink, and pale green.

5. Start with the bottom tier. Ice a side segment with one of the colors. Using your metal spatula scrape the excess over the top and sides. Ice the segment directly to the right of the first with another color. Again scrape the excess over the top and right side. On the left spread the buttercream up to and over the edge slightly. Run a hot metal spatula up the right side of the preceding segment. This should form a ridge of buttercream along the edge of the second segment. Starting in the upper left corner of the second segment, run the spatula in a downward angle to the right to cut off the excess buttercream and smooth out the segment. Remember to use the cardboard edge as your guide. Repeat this for each segment.

6. Divide the cake's top into 6 segments from corner to corner. Ice one triangle with a color. The buttercream should go up to the edge similar to the sides. Run a hot spatula along the side. This will create a lip of buttercream on top. Run the spatula across it to remove it. Scrape off the excess buttercream to the right of the triangle. Ice the triangle directly to the right of it.

Repeat for each remaining triangle. Each section will have a different fabric pattern. Pipe crazy curls, rickrack, stripes, lattice, or plaid (see pages 66–69), or stick the chocolate decorations to the soft buttercream. Glue the cardboard round supporting the cake to your base. Insert dowels to support the next tier.

7. Ice the second tier with white buttercream. While the buttercream is soft stick the buttons randomly all over the cake. Center the cake on top of the bottom tier. Insert dowels to support the top tier.

8. Finish the top tier in the same manner as the bottom tier, except the top surface will be one pattern. Center it on top of the second tier.

9. Place the spool of thread on top. Press the skewer into the cake below to hold the spool in place.

10. Place the remaining uncolored buttercream in a pastry bag with a coupler, and with a small round tip, pipe "topstitching" on all of the edges where different fabrics meet. These are made with small x's. With a petal or flat tip, finish the bottom borders with rickrack.

11. Stick the scissors on the top tier and the needle on the bottom tier. Pipe a line of thread through the needle's eye.

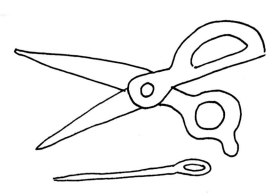

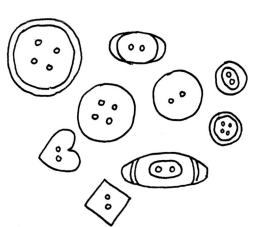

Tipsy Birthday Bash

This cake isn't just for kids, it is for anyone young at heart—perfect for the child in us all, whether we are turning thirty, forty, fifty, sixty . . . If you are looking for something a little bit wacky and totally fun that is guaranteed to be a conversation starter, look no further; the gravity-defying construction will keep your guests guessing how the cake remains standing. Despite its eye-popping appearance, this is one of the simpler multitiered cakes to make and perfection is not a requirement because a slightly loopy irregularity to the decoration only enhances its playful effect. Do play around with the colors, because the more retro you feel like getting, the better! If you like, replace the chocolate candles with real wax candles and save yourself one step.

Techniques used to make this cake: Tilted Tiered Cakes (page 121), Relief Chocolate Method (page 101), and Piping (page 66).

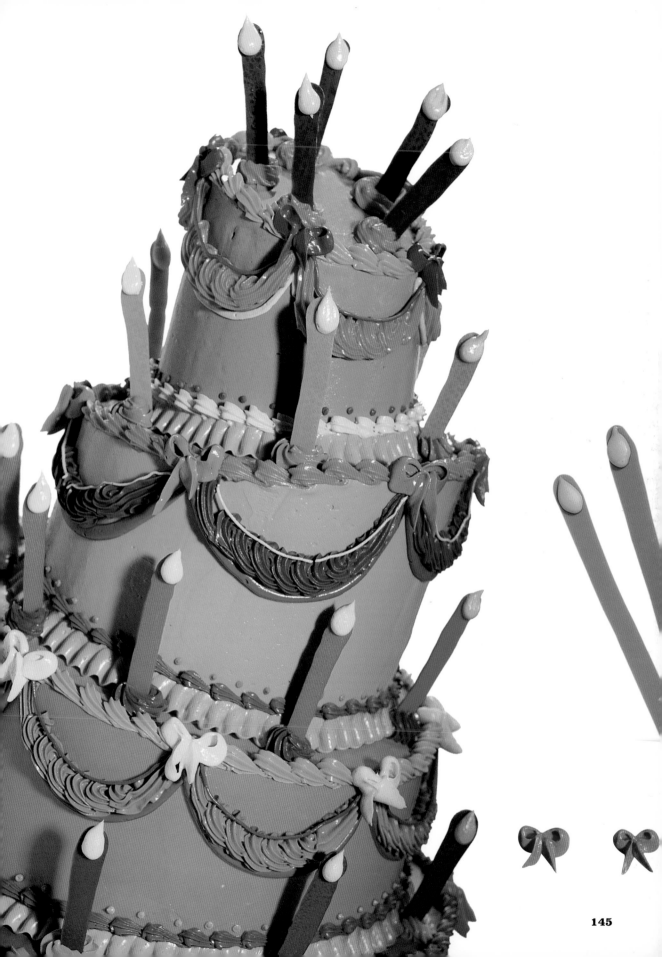

What you will need:

Cake: 4 tiers, including one 10-inch round cake, one 8-inch round cake, one 6-inch round cake, and one 4-inch round cake; 17 cups batter for Chocolate Butter Cake (page 65)

Filling: 12 cups Cookies and Cream (page 65)

Icing: 3 recipes Kaye's Buttercream (page 37) or House Buttercream (page 36)

Decoration: 4½ cups white wafer chocolate to make 35 candles

Colors: liquid gel colors in blue, violet, neon pink, orange, green, teal, and yellow, and candy colors in blue, red, yellow, green, purple, pink, and orange

Tips: #104 and #102 petal tip, #16, #17, or #18 star tip, and # 5, #6, or #7 round tip

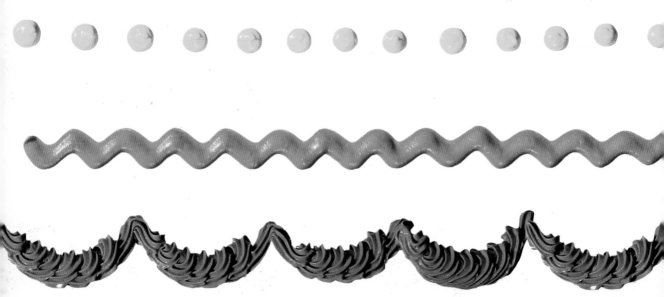

How to:

1. Melt 4½ cups white wafer chocolate. Tint the white chocolate; approximately ½ cup yellow and 1 cup each of midnight blue, neon pink, lime green, and purple. Make 4 sets of chocolate candles. The bottom tier will get 12 blue candles, the second 10 neon pink, the third 6 lime green, and the top 5 purple.

2. Bake the cakes and let them cool completely. Prepare the icing and filling. Fill and crumb coat the cakes as directed in Filling a Tilted Cake (page 33). Chill the filled cakes.

3. Using the Color Mixing Chart on page 26, prepare the colored butter-cream: approximately 5 cups midnight blue, 3 cups lime green, 1½ cups yellow, 3½ cups neon pink, 1½ cups purple, 2 cups orange, and 2 cups teal.

4. Ice the bottom tier with purple buttercream. Glue the cardboard circle supporting the cake to the center of your base. Insert dowels to support the next tier.

5. Ice the second tier with pink buttercream. Center the cake on top of the bottom tier. Insert dowels to support the next tier.

6. Ice the third tier in lime green. Center the cake on top of the second tier. Insert dowels to support the top tier.

7. Ice the top tier in teal. Center the cake on top of the third tier. Sharpen one end of a dowel the height of the finished cake and carefully hammer it through the center of all of the cakes and cardboard rounds to the base.

8. Prepare 7 pastry bags with couplers. Fill each with the seven colors previously mixed.

9. With a petal tip, pipe an orange Ruffled Ribbon Border (page 67) around the bottom edge of each tier. With a round tip, pipe a yellow or blue Shell Border (page 67) above each ruffled border. With the same tip, pipe yellow or blue Thread Swags (page 68 on each tier corresponding to the Shell Border.

10. With a star tip, pipe green Spiral Swags (page 68) and 12 Rosettes around the top of the bottom tier. Pipe teal Spiral Swags and 10 rosettes around the top of the second tier. Pipe purple Spiral Swags and 8 rosettes around the top of the third tier. Pipe pink Spiral Swags and 5 rosettes around the top of the top tier. Pipe thin Linear Swags in contrasting colors on top of the Spiral Swags.

11. With a star tip, pipe Shell Borders in contrasting colors around the top of each tier.

12. With a small petal tip, pipe bows in contrasting colors where the swags meet.

13. Choose a front for the cake, preferably a side on which the top tier is angled forward.

14. Press the candles halfway into the rosettes with the flat side facing forward.

Oh Baby

Baby showers and first birthdays are
momentous occasions that deserve a
special cake. (Of course, we believe
every occasion deserves a cake!) Because
a baby is not just a bundle of joy, but
bundles of joy, this cake is packed with
goodies, from teddy bears to safety pins. And because
becoming a parent for the first time can leave anyone a little
bit off balance, the off-kilter tilted construction should bring
a smile to the face of the mom- or dad-to-be. Pink and blue are
the obvious color choices here, but even if you know the gender
of the little one, choose a different color for each tier
as well as for the draping baby blanket to
prevent the cake from becoming too cutesy; yellow
and lavender are good choices if you prefer a
non-gender-specific cake.

Techniques used to make this cake: Tilted Tiered
Cakes (page 121), Multicolor Chocolate Method
(page 78), Advanced Chocolate Method
(page 93), and Piping (page 66).

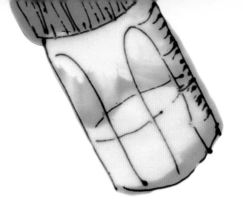

What you will need:

Cake: 2 tiers, including one 9-inch round cake and one 6-inch round cake; 9 cups batter for White Butter Cake (page 98)

Filling: 7¼ cups Raspberry Mousse (page 100)

Icing: 2 to 2½ recipes Kaye's Buttercream (page 37) or House Buttercream (page 36)

Decoration: 2 cups dark wafer chocolate and 8 cups white wafer chocolate to make 2 large mirror-image babies; 2 each bottles, rattles, blocks, bears, bunnies, pacifiers, ducks, and safety pins; 6 to 10 small babies; and 20 polka dots

Colors: liquid gel colors in sky blue, green, hot pink, and yellow, and candy colors in blue, pink, yellow, green, purple, and orange

Tips: #104, #103, or #102 petal tip; #46 or #47 basket weave tip; and #2, #4 and #7 round tips

How to:

1. Melt 2 cups dark wafer chocolate and 8 cups white wafer chocolate. Set aside 1 cup of uncolored white chocolate for detail work. Using the Color Mixing Chart on page 26, tint the remaining white chocolate: approximately ½ cup each, lavender, purple, pale pink, neon pink, yellow, light orange, mint green, lime green, sky blue, light brown, brown, and pale peach. Make the babies, bottles, bears, bunnies, ducks, blocks, pacifiers, and rattles as directed in the Multicolor and/or Advanced Chocolate Method. Trace two larger babies onto parchment paper. Turn one upside down, and one right side up. Place another sheet of parchment paper over them. Make the two babies as directed in the Multicolor Chocolate Method. Extend their legs 1 inch with chocolate.

2. Bake the cakes and let them cool completely. Prepare the filling and icing. Fill and crumb coat the cakes as directed in Filling a Tilted Cake (page 33). Chill the filled cakes.

3. Prepare the colored buttercream: 3 cups pale pink, 4 cups mint green, 1 cup pale yellow, and 2 cups baby blue.

4. Ice the bottom tier with pale pink buttercream. Adhere the cardboard round supporting the cake to your base with glue. To make the Baby Blanket, trace a wavy line around the side of the cake with a toothpick. Place the mint-green buttercream in a pastry bag with a coupler, and with a basket weave tip, pipe basket weave (see page 69) covering the top and sides up to this line. Place the yellow and pink buttercreams

in pastry bags with couplers. With a round tip, pipe yellow and pink strings hanging from the baby blanket and dots on the edge of the blanket. Insert dowels to support the top tier.

5. Ice the top tier with baby-blue buttercream. Center the cake on top of the bottom tier. Sharpen one end of a dowel the height of the finished cake and carefully hammer it through the center of all of the cakes and cardboard rounds to the base.

6. Lightly mark the position of the babies on the top tier with their legs. They should be centered with their backs facing each other. Stick a knife into the cake at these points. Carefully press the babies into the slots until their toes are resting on the icing. Fill in the empty space between them with piped confetti or flowers, using the leftover tinted buttercream.

7. With a petal tip, finish off the top and bottom tiers with a pink, yellow, and blue Ruffled Ribbon, Rickrack, and/or Crazy borders (see pages 66–69).

8. While the buttercream is soft, stick the smaller babies and polka dots around the top tier and the rest of the items around the bottom tier beneath the baby blanket.

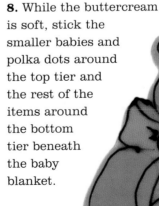

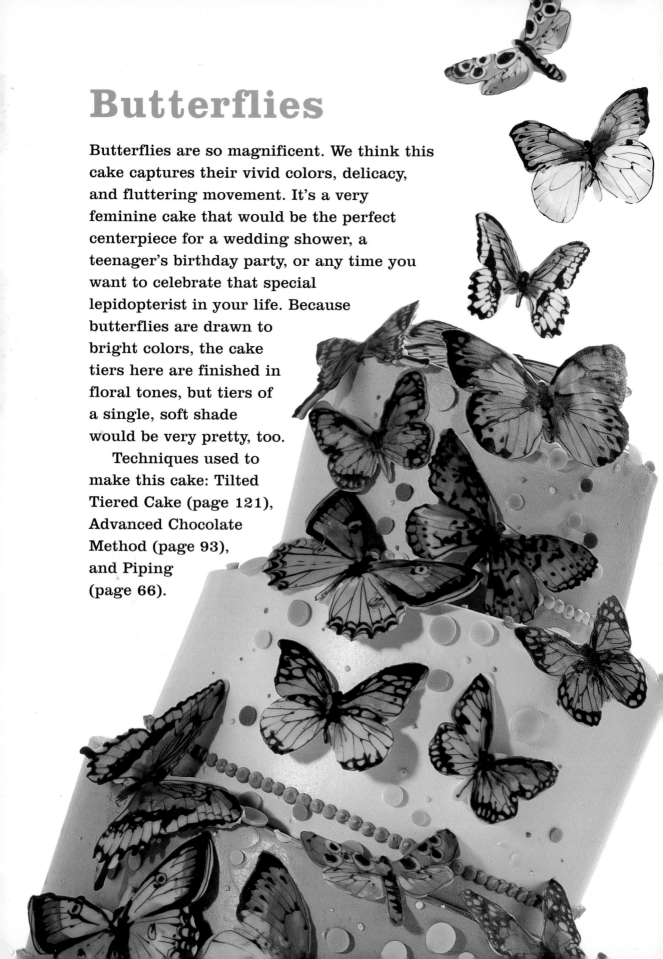

Butterflies

Butterflies are so magnificent. We think this cake captures their vivid colors, delicacy, and fluttering movement. It's a very feminine cake that would be the perfect centerpiece for a wedding shower, a teenager's birthday party, or any time you want to celebrate that special lepidopterist in your life. Because butterflies are drawn to bright colors, the cake tiers here are finished in floral tones, but tiers of a single, soft shade would be very pretty, too.

Techniques used to make this cake: Tilted Tiered Cake (page 121), Advanced Chocolate Method (page 93), and Piping (page 66).

What you will need:

Cake: 3 tiers, including one 10-inch round cake, one 8-inch round cake, and one 6-inch round cake; 16 cups batter for Banana Cake (page 86) or Chocolate Butter Cake (page 65)

Filling: 12½ cups Whipped Chocolate Ganache (page 60)

Icing: 2 recipes Kaye's Buttercream (page 37) or House Buttercream (page 36)

Decoration: 2 cups dark wafer chocolate and 8 cups white wafer chocolate to make 15 to 20 butterflies

Colors: violet, green, and yellow liquid gel colors and blue, pink, yellow, green, purple, and orange candy colors

Tips: #104, #103, or #102 petal tip and #2, #4 or #7 round tip

How to:

1. Melt 2 cups dark wafer chocolate and approximately 8 cups white wafer chocolate. Using the Color Mixing Chart on page 26, tint the white chocolate: approximately ½ cup each red-orange, orange, yellow, peach, lilac, purple, pink-purple, sky blue, periwinkle, lime green, aqua, and pale pink. Using the Advanced Chocolate Method, make a variety of butterflies. Pipe small polka dots onto a sheet of parchment paper with the leftover chocolate.

2. Bake the cakes and let them cool completely. Prepare the filling and icing. Fill and crumb coat the cakes as directed in Filling a Tilted Cake (page 33). Chill.

3. Prepare the colored buttercream; tint approximately 2 cups light lime green, 3 cups soft yellow, and 4 cups lavender.

4. Ice the bottom tier with the lavender buttercream, saving the remaining buttercream for piping. Glue the cardboard round supporting the cake to your base. Insert dowels to support the next tier.

5. Ice the second tier with the yellow buttercream, saving the remaining buttercream for piping. Center the cake on top of the bottom tier. Insert dowels to support the top tier.

6. Ice the top tier with green buttercream, again saving the remaining buttercream for piping. Center the cake

on top of the middle tier in the same manner. Sharpen one end of a dowel the height of the finished cake and carefully hammer it through the center of all of the cakes and cardboard rounds to the base.

7. Place each of the reserved butter-creams in a pastry bag with a coupler. With a petal tip, pipe a Flat Ribbon Border (page 68) around the bottom border of each tier in the matching color. Change to a round tip. On top of each Flat Ribbon pipe a dot border in a contrasting color.

8. Choose a front for the cake, preferably a side with the top tier angled forward. Pipe small dots of butter-cream on the backs of the butterflies and adhere them to the cake at different angles to form a flying cascade. Pipe small dots and stick polka dots in and around the butterfly cascade.

List of Suppliers

MAIL ORDER

Wilton Industries, Inc.
2240 West 75th Street
Woodridge, IL 60517
Phone: 800-794-5866
Website: www.wilton.com

New York Cake and Baking Distributors, Inc.
56 West 22nd Street
New York, NY 10010
Phone: 800-942-2539 or 212-675-7955

The King Arthur Flour Baker's Catalogue
Norwich, VT
Phone: 800-827-6836
Website: www.KingArthurFlour.com

The Foodcrafter's Supply Catalog
Waukon, IA
Phone:800-776-0575
Website: www.KitchenKrafts.com

WHOLESALE MAIL ORDER

Pfeil and Holing
58–15 Northern Boulevard
Woodside, NY 11377
Phone: 800-247-7955

Appendixes

THE CAKE ASSEMBLAGE CHART

The chart below provides general guidelines for how much filling and icing you will need to assemble and finish a cake with three layers in a variety of sizes. Beginners may need to prepare a bit more icing to give them a margin for error. You will find this chart especially helpful when making tiered cakes, which will require you to prepare multiple batches of both cake batter and any fillings or icings. In some cases you can simply double (or triple) the recipe as you make it. However, unless you have a very large mixer bowl, it is more likely you will need to make successive batches. Batter for 8-inch and 9-inch cakes when doubled will fit in the bowl of a 5-quart mixer, but a double recipe for a 10-inch, unless you are very careful, will not. Each recipe in this book indicates how many cups of filling you will need to make the cake exactly as shown; by referring to the recipe yields you can easily determine how many batches of each are required. That way you can adapt any recipe you like, or change the pan sizes at will.

CAKE SIZE	FILLING	RING AND CRUMB	FINAL COAT
4-inch	¾ cup	¾ cup	¾ cup
6-inch	1½ cups	1 cup	1 cup
6-inch tilted	¾ cup and 1½ cups	1¼ cup	1¼ cup
8-inch	3 cups	1½ cups	1½ cups
8-inch tilted	1½ and 2¼ cups	1¾ cups	1¾ cups
9-inch	4 cups	2 cups	2 cups
9-inch tilted	2 cups and 3 cups	2¼ cups	2¼ cups
10-inch	5 cups	2¼–2½ cups	2½ cups
10-inch tilted	2½ cups and 3½–4 cups	2½–2¾ cups	2¾ cups
12-inch	6 cups	3 cups	3 cups
12-inch tilted	3 cups and 5 cups	3½ cups	3½ cups
8-inch square	5½ cups	2½ cups	2½ cups
6-inch hexagon	2 cups	1½ cups	1½ cups
9-inch hexagon	4 cups	2½ cups	2½ cups
12-inch hexagon	7 cups	3½ cups	3½ cups
15-inch hexagon	10 cups	5 cups	5 cups

BAKING TIMES

If you are making a multitiered cake, your batter will be baked in pans of two or more sizes. Refer to the chart below to determine the proper baking time for each, based upon the pan size and the amount of batter in each.

   Any cake recipe can be baked in a single pan and then split into layers when cooled, but to avoid overbaking and to keep the cakes moist, it's generally a good idea to divide the batter among two pans. Cakes smaller than 8 inches need only one pan.

CAKE SIZE	CUPS OF batter for one pan	BAKING time in minutes	CUPS of batter for short cake/ first pan	BAKING time in minutes	CUPS of batter for taller cake/ second Pan	BAKING time in minutes
4-inch round	1–1½	18–22				
6-inch round	3	30–35				
8-inch round	5	35–40				
9-inch round	6½–7	40–45	3	20–25	3½–4	25–30
10-inch round	8–9	55–60	3½	20–25	4½–5½	35–40
8-inch square	6	40–45	2	15–20	4	25–30
6-inch hexagon			1	12–15	1	12–15
9-inch hexagon			2	15–20	2	15–20
12-inch hexagon			5	35–50	5	35–40
15-inch hexagon			4	25–30	7	40–45

SERVINGS

Here are some general rules of thumb regarding the number of servings yielded by cakes of different sizes. Wedding cake servings are usually smaller than standard servings, so we've calculated it both ways.

CAKE SIZE	SERVINGS	WEDDING SERVINGS
4-inch round	up to 4	up to 4
6-inch round	up to 8	up to 14
8-inch round	up to 12	up to 25
9-inch round	up to 18	up to 30
10-inch round	up to 25	up to 35
12-inch round	up to 35	up to 50
8-inch square	up to 18	up to 32
6-inch hexagon	up to 7	up to 12
9-inch hexagon	up to 17	up to 22
12-inch hexagon	up to 24	up to 50
15-inch hexagon	up to 44	up to 72

Index